Temperament

Tools

Tools

**Working with
Your Child's Inborn Traits**

by
Helen Neville, B.S, R.N. and
Diane Clark Johnson, C.F.L.E.

Illustrated by
Dave Garbot

Parenting Press, Inc.
Seattle, Washington

Printed in the United States of America
ISBN 1-884734-34-0 paperback
ISBN 1-884734-35-9 library binding

Edited by Carolyn J. Threadgill
Designed by Margarite Hargrave

Library of Congress Cataloguing-in-Publication Data
Neville, Helen, 1943-
    Temperament tools : working with your child's inborn traits / by
Helen Neville and Diane Clark Johnson : illustrated by Dave
Garbot.
        p.   cm.
    Includes bibliographical references and index.
    ISBN 1-884734-35-9 (lib. bdg.). -- ISBN 1-884734-34-0 (pbk.)
    1. Temperament in children.   2. Child rearing.   I. Johnson,
Diane Clark, 1960-   . II. Title.
    BF723.T53N48   1998
    649'.122--DC21   97-37466

Parenting Press, Inc.
P.O. Box 75267
Seattle, Washington 98175
www.ParentingPress.com

Contents

We dedicate this book—
to our children, who continue to teach us about
  parenting,
to Jim Cameron, Ph.D. for his generous teaching,
and to our supportive spouses, John and Rob.

Foreword

With a bit of imagination, children can be compared to highways. Some are easy: flat, wide, straight lanes with comfortable, gradual turns and ample shoulders. Others seem designed by the Marquis de Sade: unexpected pot holes; slick, sharp curves; abrupt entrances and exits; no shoulders; no passing zones.

When your child is born, how do you know whether you are going to have a relaxed drive along an easy highway or a hair-raising ride down a steep hill?

In the past, we generally believed that all children were basically the same at birth. One map served as a guide to all children. Now we know that different children develop along different developmental routes, depending on their temperament, their behavioral style. We also know that parents need better maps to be able to follow their children and try to ease the way around some of the difficult spots.

First, you need a good mirror that will reflect a clear image of your child's temperament. Second, with that reflection in mind, you need a good road map to tell you what roadblocks lie ahead for *your* child. Third, you need a set of guideposts that will work with each upcoming roadblock. Finally, you need to know something about your own temperament and preferred parenting style, so you can pick from a set of guideposts the approach that fits *you*.

From years of temperament counseling directly with parents, individually and in groups, Helen Neville and Diane Johnson have developed all the tools you may need. They will help you select for your journey the individual tools that will work best for you as you pick up that map and travel with your child down the parenting highway.

—James Cameron, Ph.D.
The Preventive Ounce,
Oakland, California

Gifts from Birth, Inborn Traits

Most parents know that children are different from one another from the day they are born. Not so long ago, researchers believed all children were *born* the same, but turned out differently because of how they were raised. What *especially* mattered was how their parents treated them. Newer research proves what parents knew all along—children really are different from birth. Moreover, they remain different no matter how they are parented.

Two researchers, Dr. Stella Chess and Dr. Alexander Thomas, have identified nine major differences among children. These differences, called *temperament traits,* show how each child deals with the world.

Temperament is responsible for a great deal of behavior. For example, some babies are born with very sensitive bodies. They are more sensitive to pain, clothing textures, flavors of different foods, and temperature. Some children are very persistent from birth. They keep trying things over and over, even if they don't get or can't do what they want at first. Other children are quick to move on.

The traits babies are born with are also seen in adults. Active toddlers usually become active adults. Some traits, however, may modify with time. Babies who are low in approach (also called cautious, shy, or slow to warm) can, as they grow older, learn to feel more comfortable in new situations and around new people.

Understanding your child's inborn temperament makes your job as a parent easier. Imagine that your new baby is like a mysterious island. What you need is a map of that island. A knowledge of temperament provides the map that makes exploring easier and more enjoyable. When you know what to expect, you can travel with more confidence.

Dr. James Cameron, a leader in temperament research, has continued the work of Drs. Chess and Thomas. He has studied the temperament traits of *thousands* of babies. Dr. Cameron has identified the clusters of problems that are common to different sets of temperament traits and has explored how best to work with each one. He has provided parents with a map to their unique child. This book is based on his research.

You might wonder how children and adults can be so different from one another if there are only nine basic temperament traits. The answer lies in the varied combinations of the nine traits. Think of personality in terms of a layer cake. The bottom layer is temperament. Other layers are composed of the child's growth and development, relationships with family, experiences in school and community, friendships, and all the adventures of living. The purpose of this book is to help you understand the bottom layer, *temperament*.

Temperament has been studied all around the world. In every culture, children are born with a whole range of different temperament clusters.

Temperament helps parents avoid blame and guilt. There are no "good" or "bad" kids in temperament terms. Just as bicycles, cars, and airplanes each have their own special advantages and disadvantages, so it is with temperament traits. With practice, parents can learn to appreciate and work with their child's traits, whatever these may be. *They learn not to blame* their children for their temperaments.

Likewise, there are no "good" or "bad" parents in the world of temperament. Just as it takes more skill to manage an airplane than a bicycle, it takes more skill and knowledge to manage children with certain temperament traits than others. Some parents simply have a tougher job because their kids came into the world with a more challenging combination of traits. *These parents need not feel guilty* because they have a harder time.

Parents who understand temperament learn to prevent behavior problems by responding appropriately to what their kids need. Different temperaments call for different handling and different environments. When the parenting style and the environment fit the child, he or she can thrive and grow. In this book you will find many tools for working with your child's temperament.

What Makes My Child Tick?

Parents generally know their children better than anyone else. You will be able to fill in the temperament chart below by thinking carefully about your baby or young child. One baby always cried and arched her back whenever she was in an infant seat. At the same age, her little brother sat wide-eyed and still in the same seat, causing the pediatrician to remark, "Some babies devour the world with their eyes." If you are the parent of more than one child, you may have seen such differences just a few days after birth. However, many babies need a few months to settle in. Their true temperament traits become more reliably visible at four months of age.

Temperament Chart

For each of the traits that follow, read the descriptions and consider whether your child's temperament falls at one extreme or another or is somewhere in the middle of the line. Many children are middle of the road in most traits, but may be extreme in one or two. More rarely (and more challengingly), some are extreme in several, or most, traits. Notice that there are extremes at *each end* of each temperament line. Sometimes it helps to ask your partner, the child's grandparents, a day care provider or teacher, or someone else who knows the child well, how they see the child.

1. Activity

Low energy: This infant relaxes in the infant seat and high chair. He sleeps peacefully. As a toddler he snuggles contentedly on your lap or sits with toys in the center of the room. Arms and legs flop limply or gently; he cooperates with dressing. As a preschooler, he usually moves slowly and uses hands more than feet. He manipulates small toys, enjoys art work, puzzles, or building.

High energy: This infant kicked vigorously before she was born and usually walks early. Even when asleep, she wiggles across the crib. Arms and legs fly during diaper changes. As a toddler, she hates being imprisoned in car seat, stroller, or high chair. As a preschooler, she talks fast and moves fast. She loves large spaces for play, dances while watching videos, and wiggles while listening to stories.

Mark your child's activity level with an X anywhere along the scale.

Activity
Low energy   High energy

|____|____|____|____|____|____|____|____|

2. Adaptability

High: This infant glides comfortably through daily transitions—waking up, falling asleep, being picked up, bathed, or put down. As a toddler, she quickly settles into new situations and accepts limits. She drinks milk from either the red cup or the blue one. As a preschooler, she gets along easily with playmates and goes with the flow when family plans change.

Low: This infant may fuss on waking, near the end of each day, and before falling asleep. He doesn't like having his face washed and may even get upset by eye contact. His body stiffens when he's picked up or moved. As a toddler, he fusses during dressing and has trouble falling asleep, especially in new places. He has trouble settling into new child care arrangements. He fights limits by repeating the same misbehavior. As a preschooler, he gets upset when plans change, or when you cut his toast the wrong way. He disagrees with playmates and bosses them around.

Mark your child's adaptability level with an X anywhere along the scale.

Adaptability

High   Low

|_____|_____|_____|_____|_____|_____|_____|

3. Approach to new things

High: This infant tries out new foods and automatically reaches toward new toys and pets. As a toddler, he immediately climbs into a new bed, smiles at the new sitter, or joins a new play group. He's attracted to all new things, whether they are safe or dangerous. This preschooler is always ready to visit a new friend, a new house, a new park, or a new school.

Cautious: This infant wrinkles her nose at the smell of a new food or spits it out. She turns away or cries when a stranger approaches. She watches others play with a new toy before trying it personally. As a toddler and preschooler, she hides silently behind you when you greet someone new. She's sure that the old bed, house, or school is better than any new one could be.

Mark your child's approach level with an X anywhere along the scale.

Approach to new things

High   Cautious

|_____|_____|_____|_____|_____|_____|_____|

4. Frustration reaction

Persistent: This infant patiently waits for milk. Later she practices standing and walking despite the tumbles. As a toddler, she entertains herself by practicing new games and skills repeatedly or with one approach after another. Her inborn motto is, "If at first you don't succeed, try and try again." As a preschooler, she gains new skills because she instinctively practices. She patiently works to surmount the hurdles of life.

Easily discouraged or frustrated: This infant demands milk instantly and is upset if it flows too fast or slow. As a toddler, he quickly loses interest in a toy or activity that doesn't work easily, so he browses from one thing to another. As a preschooler, he throws the blocks that toppled over, or won't try the scissors because they didn't cut the paper yesterday. He demands help getting dressed because it's too hard to do alone. Your necessary limits make him angry instantly. He loves watching videos because "success" is guaranteed.

Mark your child's level of frustration reaction with an X anywhere along the scale.

Frustration reaction　　　　　　　　　　Easily discouraged
Persistent　　　　　　　　　　　　　　　　　　or frustrated

|_____|_____|_____|_____|_____|_____|_____|

5. Intensity of emotions

Mellow: This infant silently smiles his joy or frowns his distress. As a toddler, his body remains relaxed even as emotions parade across his face. As a preschooler, he can stand quietly and tell his playmate that his feelings were hurt. His strong feelings, which he has rarely, fade quickly and automatically into calmness.

Dramatic: This infant squeals with pleasure or screams with distress. As a toddler, she may bite when she's happy or angry. She loves or hates bright lights, dressing, bath time, each toy and person. She expresses feelings with her whole body. Her tantrums are long and loud. As a preschooler, she reacts strongly to excitement, praise, criticism, or disappointment. She may slug a playmate before calming down enough to use her words. There are no small feelings. Everything is fabulous or horrible.

Mark your child's emotional intensity level with an X anywhere along the scale.

Intensity
Mellow　　　　　　　　　　　　　　　　　　　　　Dramatic

|_____|_____|_____|_____|_____|_____|_____|

6. Mood

Sunny: This infant wakes with a smile and settles to sleep with a contented sigh. She smiles on the changing table, in your arms, and in the stroller. She coos at strangers and the doctor. She tolerates life's momentary tiredness, disappointment, pain, and discipline, then moves on to more pleasant things.

Somber: This infant fusses when tired or going to sleep and also when waking up. He fusses about food, dressing, and bathing, unless everything is "just so." As a toddler, he scowls at the sitter and the doctor. He protests new playmates and anything else that's unexpected. As a preschooler, he notices and complains about all of life's disappointments and imperfections.

Mark your child's mood as sunny or somber with an X anywhere along the scale.

Mood
Sunny   Somber

|_____|_____|_____|_____|_____|_____|_____|_____|

Note: *Mood* is a complex trait. While a tendency to be sunny or somber is inborn, mood is greatly affected by other traits that are also present. Children who are cautious (low approach) or easily frustrated are often unhappy because of the effects of their underlying traits, regardless of their natural mood.

Mood also seems to reflect how well the child's environment fits him. For example, a cautious child who is repeatedly pushed too hard and fast into new experiences will be unhappy. One of the goals of this book is to help you establish a "good fit" between your child and his environment.

7. Regularity

Predictable: This infant has an internal alarm clock—he wakes and gets hungry and tired at the same times each day. As a toddler, he's automatically on a schedule. You can predict when he'll be most active each day and when tomorrow's poop will come. Because he's sleepy at the same time each night, it's easy to establish a bedtime routine that works like a charm.

Irregular: One day this infant wakes early, the next day she sleeps late. She takes long naps and short naps. There's no predicting her schedule. As a toddler, she eats three small meals some days and five big ones on others. As a preschooler, she may get unpredictably grouchy because no one expected her to be tired or hungry at that moment. She's not sleepy at the same time each night.

Mark your child's regularity with an X anywhere along the scale.

Regularity
Predictable   Irregular

8. Sensitivity

Low: This infant sleeps through parties and plane rides. One brand of food tastes the same as another, and a cotton-poly shirt feels the same as pure cotton. This toddler may ignore the scratch on her knee, the dull ache in her ear, the load in her diaper, or the fact that there is about to be a load in her diaper. As a preschooler, she may not particularly notice the emotions on people's faces or in their voices.

High: This infant wakes with noise or sudden light. He notices everything—gentle touch, temperature, textures, and smells. He notices your new glasses or a haircut. A dry diaper feels different than a wet one. His ear may be uncomfortable before the doctor can see any sign of an ear infection. He gets overwhelmed when too much information piles into his brain at one time. As a preschooler, he notices tiny sounds and faint smells. He reads others' emotions easily and reacts to even mild approval and disapproval.

Mark your child's sensitivity with an X anywhere along the scale.

Sensitivity
Low   High

Summary

You may want to copy each of your child's scores onto the temperament poster on page 121 so you can get an overview of your child's temperament. In general (not always), the more the marks fall toward the middle or the left, the easier the parent's job. In general, the more the marks fall to the right extreme, the more challenging the parent's job.

Note: If you are familiar with the research of Drs. Chess and Thomas, you know that they include a ninth scale, distractibility. Though it is an important trait in theory, we have not included it because it is much less useful than other traits in predicting likely *behavior issues.*

Now that you have a picture of your child's temperament, take a look to see if there are any surprises. Most parents have a preconceived notion of what their child might be like. Sometimes the notion doesn't fit the reality. In that case, it is wise to spend some time acknowledging that your child is different from what you expected and unique in ways you didn't anticipate. If you hoped for a dramatic artist and got instead an introspective scholar (or vice versa), you will want to substitute a more temperamentally appropriate dream of your child's future.

Behavior that Goes with Temperament Clusters

As we mentioned earlier, Dr. James Cameron mapped out the behavior issues that commonly occur with different clusters of temperament traits. Another way to figure out what makes your child unique is to look at the *behavior* of your child to see if it fits any of the clusters Dr. Cameron identified. Look at the lists of behaviors below and pick the one (or several) that best describes the challenges you face with your child. You can see that each succeeding list represents a more challenging child.

A page number appears after each cluster, and you may go directly to that chapter for help, or you may prefer to read Chapter Three first.

 This baby or child generally eats, sleeps, and accepts limits fairly easily. In many ways, this is an "easy" child, though there may be a few recurrent issues—like getting into things. If your child doesn't fit any of the following clusters, come back to this one. See page 31.

This low energy child is not assertive. He calmly looks for other amusement after a playmate snatches his toy. When playmates announce, "Let's go build with the blocks!" this child climbs out of the sandbox to comply. Can be taken advantage of by other children. See page 41.

This low energy child dawdles and forgets; is shy and dependent; has trouble leaving parents. He or she seems so clingy and fragile that parents wonder if such children will be living at home for the next thirty years. See page 45.

 Whether high or low energy, this child refuses to join activities or eat new foods. May, however, bite people. Has difficulty leaving parents. Parents worry that he'll never make friends, have a life of his own, or eat a well-balanced diet. See page 53.

 This child, whether high or low energy, is a strong-willed perfectionist who wants everything "just so." Is often too excited to get to sleep and wakes repeatedly. Has trouble leaving parents. Feelings get hurt easily. Has long, loud, or frequent temper tantrums: argues, bites, hits. May hold breath, vomit, or bang head when upset. Visits to the doctor are difficult. See page 63.

 This fast-moving child won't sit still to eat, dashes away from parents; is friendly to everyone. Demands a lot of help and then refuses it; has temper tantrums and a short attention span; suffers boredom; may stutter. Has an eye for trouble, is the class clown, blames others unfairly, and has trouble getting along with friends. See page 83.

This active child doesn't like to cuddle or wear shoes, a hat, or a bib, and eats few foods, demands to feed self. Talks too much or too loudly, is bossy, doesn't pay attention. Trips are terribly difficult. See page 105.

This high energy child has many of the behaviors of the previous three. If you are therefore having trouble deciding which chapter to pick, turn first to page 117.

Which child above shows the issues you struggle with the most? Some children fit more than one temperament cluster, so are described in several different chapters. Do you see similar extremes in the temperament traits of your child and the story child of the chapter you chose? The tools given in that chapter will be particularly useful to you and your child.

If your child has a moderate temperament generally, but is extreme in one trait, you will find help in Chapter 4, pages 33–39.

Temperament Tango, Parent & Child Together

An important part of understanding a child's behavior is how the parents' and the child's temperaments interact. On the temperament chart you filled in for your child, mark *your* position on each of the nine temperament traits.

As you look at some traits, you may feel a significant difference between your "natural" self and how you currently live your life. If so, mark "I" for inborn and "C" for current. As we observed earlier, one can learn ways to behave that are contrary to one's inborn temperament. It is still important to know what your basic temperament is.

When parent and child share the same temperament trait or when they are opposites, problems can occur. In this chapter, we highlight the most likely interactions between you and your child, based on the charts you filled in for each. Find the traits below where either you or your child is high or low and read what you can do to improve your relationship.

1. Activity

Child, low energy
Parent, low energy
You share quiet, slower paced activities. Few problems arise.
- *For your health, exercise together gently. Go for walks together.*
- *Encourage exercise with younger children. Your child may feel more competent than with age-mates who are active or athletically gifted.*

Parent, high energy
To you, your child seems lazy. She tires quickly and doesn't like sports. She is unlikely to excel in athletics.
- *Respect her slower pace.*
- *Listen to people who point out her other special abilities.*
- *Jog while you push her stroller or jog around the sandbox she's playing quietly in.*
- *Get child care so you can go out for the exercise you need.*

Child, high energy
Parent, high energy
You understand this child's need to move. One active three-year-old could jog a mile with his six-foot father. Of course, even active parents can get worn out by active children!
- *Enjoy being active with your child.*
- *Cultivate some lower energy friends to avoid overexertion.*

Parent, low energy
Think of a time when you *really* needed to get to the bathroom. Remember how your body demanded that you move? Imagine your body always being that anxious to get somewhere. That's how your child feels.
- *Remind yourself that your child needs to move as much as you need to rest or do quiet activities.*
- *Arrange part of your house to be safe for active play with wheel toys, bouncy horse, balls to throw, cushions to jump on, etc.*
- *Find safe, fenced playgrounds.*
- *Line up active relatives, sitters, other children, and child care workers who match your child's energy level.*

2. Adaptability

Child, high
Parent, high
Living together is relatively easy because you both go with the flow. Few problems arise.

Parent, low
Your flexible child may adapt quickly to your more settled ways. However, if he has to do *all* the adapting, he may resent you.
- *As a concerned parent, push yourself to adapt to your child as well.*

Child, low
Parent, low
Life would be easier with a more adaptable (flexible) child! You are both low in adaptability, but you are the mature adult. That puts the burden to adapt on you.
- *Establish routines that you both can live with. Life is easier with a plan.*
- *Keep in touch with parents of older children. Then when your child reaches a new developmental stage, you'll feel better prepared.*

Parent, high
You adjust more easily than your child. The problem with this is that you may eventually become resentful because you feel like you give in all the time. For example, your child wants you to snuggle until she falls asleep. How long are you genuinely willing to stay with her?
- *Hold the line on things that are personally important to you, which may mean snuggling for fifteen minutes, no longer.*
- *Set aside time to take care of your needs.*
- *Be kind and consistent, knowing that your child will adjust in time.*

3. Approach to new things

Child, high
Parent, high
You and your child are both attracted to all that is new and different.
- *Model exploring safely. For example, there is a strange dog nearby. Talk to its owner to find out if it's usually friendly. Invite your child to notice if the dog's tail is wagging, or whether its ears are laid back.*

Parent, cautious
This is a hard temperament combination. Either you feel frightened by your child's adventurous spirit, or she feels imprisoned because of your caution.
- *Talk with more adventuresome parents to see how they view your child's behavior before you set limits that may be overly cautious.*
- *Practice imagining this child surrounded by a protective, golden light. This self-talk will keep you calmer.*

———————

Child, cautious
Parent, cautious
If you are or were painfully cautious and shy, you want your child to feel more comfortable.
- *Prepare her ahead of time for new experiences.*
- *Know that she needs to study new situations before she steps in.*
- *Help her learn in small steps how to join the group or do a new activity.*
- *Be patient and understanding when she doesn't want to join the crowd or do something new.*
- *Continue to offer new opportunities at a pace that builds her confidence.*

Parent, high
When you are naturally adventuresome, it's hard to have a child who is cautious. Imagine visiting Mars tomorrow—you'd be greatly excited and also concerned about safety. Your child feels the same concern when first at the beach or in a room of new people.
- *Let him move into new adventures at his own pace. He'll be much more likely to feel courageous if he knows you support him in a sympathetic manner.*

4. Frustration reaction

Child, persistent
Parent, persistent
Both you and your child push through difficulty. When projects don't work at first, you both keep going to see them through. When you have a difference of opinion, you're both naturally inclined to keep looking for solutions. Appreciate this valuable trait you share.

Parent, easily discouraged or frustrated
This child will continually wear you down and push you into corners. It's harder for you than for other parents to enforce necessary rules calmly and repeatedly because you don't like frustration.

- *Pick only one or two important rules to teach at a time. That way, you'll see results and become less discouraged.*
- *Put a check on the calendar each time you enforce a limit. Plan how you might reward yourself when you get five or fifteen checks.*
- *Remind yourself that the harder you work in the beginning to enforce this rule every time, the faster your child will learn.*

Child, easily discouraged or frustrated
Parent, easily discouraged or frustrated

Both you and your child get upset or back off quickly from frustrating situations. It will be harder for you than for other parents to be around this needy, demanding child because you yourself become frustrated quickly.

- *Ask for the help of family, friends, and other parents with children. It is not necessary to do everything alone. Both you and your child can benefit from the care and assistance of others.*

Parent, persistent

It's hard for you to imagine why your child reacts so differently to frustration than you do. For the child who is easily frustrated, many of life's routine goals lie at the bottom of a 12-foot swimming pool. During the dive to fetch them, their importance vanishes. The need for air suddenly overpowers any earlier commitment to the goal, so she backs off, either discouraged or angry. She needs a patient parent to help her use a long handled net, or to drain the pool. Otherwise she may stick with goals that float accessibly on the surface and never obtain those on the bottom.

- *Expect her to back off when the going gets tough. Assume she will need help to follow through.*
- *Use your persistence to help her break goals into small, manageable pieces.*
- *Be patient and supportive while she learns to manage frustration.*

5. Intensity of emotions

Child, mellow
Parent, mellow

You make an easy-going, mellow pair!

Parent, dramatic

Your intensity may unintentionally influence the feelings or behavior of your mellow child.

- *Listen carefully to your child, allowing her to tell you about things in her own way.*
- *Resist your urge to interpret or add to your child's account.*
- *When you talk with her about her life, be interested and calm. Monitor your excitement and distress so that your intensity doesn't overpower hers. Otherwise, by comparison, her emotions will feel insignificant. Then she may learn to hide her excitement so that she can keep it for herself. Further, if you're always greatly upset by your child's pain, she becomes obliged to "take care" of both the original problem and her upset parent. Unfortunately, she may conceal her pain so that she will have only one problem to manage.*

Child, dramatic
Parent, dramatic
When you are loud and upset, your child automatically becomes more so. The level of intensity can quickly spiral out of control.
- *When you are upset, stop talking and take two deep breaths before you say another word.*
- *Speak slowly and quietly. Keep body movements small.*
- *When you can't control how you express the intensity of your feelings, step away from your child and go somewhere to calm down.*

Parent, calm
Your calm manner helps your child stay calm. Don't be frightened or controlled by her high intensity.
- *When your child is falling apart, calmly report back to her, "I see how upset you are."*
- *When your child feels heard and understood, her intensity will calm. Try reporting a time to her when you felt a similar way.*

6. Mood

Mood is affected by other traits. It is not useful to include it in this discussion of how parent's and child's temperaments work together.

7. Regularity

Child, predictable
Parent, predictable
You'll work together like the parts of a well-oiled machine!

Parent, irregular
This child puts you on a schedule. His body works according to a natural clock.

▪ *Set an alarm clock to remind yourself when to start a meal preparation or begin the bedtime routine.*

▪ *Adapt to your child's schedule. As he becomes more able to take care of himself, you'll be able to go back to your less regular ways.*

―――――――――

Child, irregular
Parent, irregular
You are both spontaneous and inclined to eat and sleep according to random body signals, not to the clock. Such a "hang loose" lifestyle works fine unless your child is also low in adaptability. Then he may be fussy because he never knows what's coming next.

▪ *If needed, provide routine and regularity so that your child feels secure.*

Parent, predictable
You're probably used to living by the clock, but your child isn't.

▪ *Because your child's schedule is unpredictable, watch her signals to see when she needs to eat and sleep.*

▪ *Some irregular children don't notice they are hungry. They just get grouchy. If so, keep nutritious snacks within their reach. To avoid power struggles, don't push your child to eat. Instead, invite, "I wonder if you'd feel better if you had a snack."*

8. Sensitivity

Child, low
Parent, low
Both you and your child may find it difficult to know how the other feels. Most of the time you get along just fine. Sometimes you may get into arguments that startle you because neither of you knew the other was upset.

▪ *Ask your child intermittently, "How are you feeling?"*

▪ *Teach her words to describe her feelings.*

Parent, high
You live in a world that your child *cannot* understand. You may feel battered by the noise, commotion, and mess he creates.

▪ *Accept him as he is and take care of yourself, too. For example, wear earplugs to block out some of his noise instead of nagging him to be quiet.*

▪ *Decide what areas of the house he can mess up and which he cannot.*

▪ *Play your favorite music to block out some of the background noise.*

■ *Avoid feeling like your child doesn't care about you or anyone else. Help him notice others' feelings, body language, and tones of voice.*

Child, high
Parent, high
You have the good fortune to understand where the other is coming from. Be aware that your feelings may easily blend or resonate. When one feels bad, the other may automatically feel guilty.

■ *Speak up clearly and specifically when you are annoyed so that painful feelings don't float around unresolved. Teach your child to do the same.*

■ *Practice imagining a shield that separates your feelings from your child's.*

Parent, low
Your child lives in a very different world than you do—full of sensations that you barely notice.

■ *Honor her sensitivity and believe what she tells you about her world and how she feels.*

■ *Learn from her how to notice more what others are feeling.*

Pulu Puppy
The Child of Moderate Temperament

Pulu Puppy is the child most parents hope for. Without our realizing it, she is the child most of us *expect* to have: a precious being full of joy and occasional tears. She alternates between excitedly exploring her world and snuggling with Mom or Dad to enjoy her favorite story. Early on, Pulu says what she wants with a look or a pointing finger. As she grows older, her requests come politely or excitedly, seldom unpleasantly. When Mom is busy, she complains, but can wait. When something doesn't work at first, she automatically tries again, and then may ask for help. She learns new rules after just a few repetitions. She usually meets disappointment with a sad face or whining, only occasionally with screaming and tantrums. Pulu Puppy is easy to live with and easy to love.

Child shows: Middle of the scale on all temperament traits

🐘 Keys to Living with the Child of Moderate Temperament

Just because Pulu has a moderate temperament doesn't mean it's easy to be her parent. She is clear about her likes and dislikes. Pulu needs what all children need:

❖ **Acceptance of stages of development.** The demanding two's and feisty four's are especially full of ups and downs.

❖ **Secure home.** Provide clear, consistent rules, so she can learn what to expect.

❖ **Support for personal growth.** Pulu needs love and support in expressing her feelings, understanding who she is, and making the best of her abilities.

❖ **Support when her family suffers stress.** Pulu needs her parents to resolve their own personal problems in order to be better parents. She needs support during stressful times—new house, new baby, new day care or school; or poverty, divorce, family illness, or domestic violence.

❖ **Time.** Despite her parents' busy schedules in a culture that offers precious little support to the essential job of parenting, Pulu needs attention from her parents.

👥 Parent Care

Early on, Pulu's mom got frustrated with other parents who complained, "It's so hard being a parent!" Pulu's mom suggested, "If you'd just be calm and consistent, your child would be calm and cooperative like Pulu." Some parents resented her suggestions. As Pulu's mom learned about inborn temperament, she realized that other children really can be much more difficult. She gradually learned to empathize. She also felt lucky that she had an easy child like Pulu.

📝 Common Behavior Issues

❖ **Discipline.** Mom felt proud when Pulu practiced standing and crawling. But about eleven months, she started practicing things that were bothersome, like climbing on the coffee table and banging cupboard doors. To help Pulu learn what she may do, Mom gives two choices and a consequence: "Pulu, you may crawl on the floor or climb on the pillows. If you climb on the coffee table, I will take you off." Dad put baby locks on the cupboard doors and gives Pulu pots to bang. Pulu's parents know that practicing is the way to learn new skills and build self-esteem. Besides, while Pulu practices, they can do their chores.

❖ **Sleep.** At five months Pulu suddenly began to have trouble getting to sleep at night. Her day had been so interesting, it was hard to slow down! Mom and Dad changed to calm activities before bedtime. Pulu loved to swing in the air, but Dad decided to play that game earlier in the evening. Pulu's parents chose a regular bedtime routine—bath, snuggling, and songs. Soon, Pulu was falling asleep easily again.

At six months, Pulu started waking at 2 a.m. Mom offered a pacifier, her favorite blanket, and a reassuring pat. After a few more nights, Mom just went to her door and said, "You're okay. It's time to go back to sleep." Pulu cried for a few minutes each night. Mom also decided to wake her for a late snack at 11 p.m. before she went to bed. She gradually gave Pulu smaller amounts of milk. Within a few weeks, Pulu was sleeping through the night again. Around eight months, Pulu gave up her morning nap. Pulu usually sleeps easily and soundly. When she is teething, or her schedule changes because of vacations or exciting visitors, she needs extra help to settle down and fall asleep.

Moderate Children with One Temperament Extreme

Some children of generally easy temperament have one temperament trait that is extreme. The challenges their parents face revolve around that trait. For example, an easy child who is highly active may be easy in all regards except that it takes a great deal of energy to keep up with her. To avoid exhaustion, her parent or care giver will need to rest when she does (even if that means the child who won't nap plays in her crib with toys and books long enough for her parent to rest).

In this section of this chapter, we highlight a few of the behavior challenges associated with extremes of each trait. Look for the trait which showed up as an extreme on your child's profile to see how to handle some common issues. The traits are listed in alphabetical order.

Activity, high energy

✦ **Dependent, clingy**. Very active children are usually outgoing and independent. If your child is not her usual self, she may be getting sick or reacting to family stress. Problems between her parents can change this child's more typically outgoing behavior. After she has been especially excited and on the go for a few days, she may cling tightly for a day or two in order to reconnect with you.

✦ **Discipline**. Around seven or eight months of age, active babies meet their first big contradiction in life. Until then, Mom and Dad almost always supported new adventures. Dad smiled when baby first held a bottle alone. Mom clapped the first time baby rolled over and started to crawl. Suddenly, however, adults frown or get upset with some new adventures, like crawling into the dirty fireplace, or tasting dust balls from under the sofa. What has happened to supportive Mom and Dad? Surely there is a mistake. Baby thinks, "I'll try that fireplace again to see if they smile and clap this time." He's not challenging your authority. He's learning new rules for living. Lucky are the children whose parents childproof the house, yard, and car and calmly enforce the same limits again and again until baby learns the new rule.

✦ **Eating**. Around seven to eight months, active babies want to be more in charge of mealtime. Some eat slowly. Between one nibble and the next, they want to finger paint with food, or practice drumming on the tray with a spoon. Plan to eat your own meal or do kitchen chores while this child eats. Other children eat quickly.

Active children nibble and graze throughout the day. They tend to eat small meals and frequent snacks. Trust their bodies to tell them when they need to eat. Avoid fights about food. When they drop food from the high chair, you might offer a toy for these physics experiments. Or just assume the meal is over.

✦ **Fearfulness**. Active children may suddenly become more fearful around nine or ten months of age. They may be afraid of heights, or noises, or unexpected events. This phenomenon may be related to new growth in parts of the brain. Generally, such fearfulness passes in a few weeks as things become more familiar.

✦ **No!** Some high energy children learn "No!" and "Don't!" at eleven or twelve months of age. They may practice this new power tool while being bathed or dressed. They may simply be playing. Or "No!" may signal the beginning of new independence, just as walking does. If you have time, go along with your child and let her enjoy her power. If you have a schedule to meet, go ahead and do what you need to do, even if she objects.

✣ **Sibling rivalry.** High energy children are attracted to older children who have the skills they want to learn. They can pester an older brother or sister unmercifully. Help the older child set reasonable limits. Make sure an older, quieter brother or sister has some peaceful space. In a small house, you might let the quiet child use your bedroom during the day.

✣ **Sleep.** At seven to eight months, many active babies start waking during the night. They may be teething or have an ear infection. Or they simply wake up and think, "This is a great time to practice sitting, crawling, or standing." Let them practice on their own so you can get your sleep. If their activity disturbs your sleep, move the crib to another room, if you haven't already done so.

Around eleven or twelve months, many active youngsters learn how to climb out of their cribs. To avoid falls, put the crib mattress at its lowest position. Or childproof the room and put the crib mattress on the floor. Close the door for safety, or put a baby gate at the door. (If necessary, use two gates, one on top of the other.)

✣ **Standing all the time.** Around nine or ten months, when active children first learn to stand, they don't want to sit down! They prefer to stand while eating, getting diapers changed, and when in bed. They may wake and stand up during the night, before they know how to sit down again. Fortunately, they soon learn how to sit down. At this age, they're more able to cooperate when standing up. They may eat better standing by a low table than when forced to sit in a high chair. This is normal behavior for this temperament. Once standing is no longer so new and exciting, they will learn to sit for short periods. (Tip: Immediately stand your child up after the nurse gives a shot. He'll usually feel much better.)

For more help, see the pages noted here:

Activity, low energy

✤ **Eating**. Some quiet youngsters want to start feeding themselves around six months of age. Others don't even want to hold their own bottles long after they are able! Go with the flow on this and avoid struggles about eating. The problem will take care of itself if left alone.

Adaptability, low

For more help, see the pages noted here:
Child care/Preschool, pages 67-68
Discipline, pages 70-71
Doctor's visits, page 72
Separation, pages 74-75
Sleep, pages 49-50, 57-58, 75-76, 98-100
Stubborn, page 76
Toilet training, pages 78-79
Weaning, page 80

Adaptability, high

✤ **Bumps and bruises**. Like all children, fast adapting ones fall while learning to stand. But children with high adaptability often get up and try again without even stopping to cry. Put mats or rugs at their favorite practicing places, or they may silently collect bumps and bruises.

Approach, cautious

✤ **Dependence**. Expect these children to become more whiny, clingy, and dependent when they learn new things. Whether they are learning to walk, starting a new school, moving to a new home, or adjusting to a new sibling, expect two steps forward, one step back. If you push them away and urge them to be more independent before they are ready, they will become more clingy. Independence returns sooner if they get the support and reassurance they need, for as long as they need it.

For more help, see the pages noted here: 45–52.

Approach, high

✤ **Boredom**. High approach children may be bored quickly once things become familiar. Give them lots of safe opportunities to explore. As they reach ages three or four years, teach safety rules. Do things together so that you can teach them how to do things safely. Rather than say, "Don't ever light matches!" say, "If you want to light matches, tell me and we'll do it together. Always do this with an adult."

✤ **Gets into everything.** These natural explorers reach out and touch everything—your hair, glasses, telephone cord, lamps, pets, and plants. Childproof the house, yard, and car thoroughly! Keep your grocery cart in the center of the store aisle. If their energy and intensity are moderate, teach them how to touch gently: "Touch it but don't move it." Thus, they can satisfy their curiosity without causing harm. If they are intense and can't control their bodies, encourage them to "touch" only with their eyes.

Frustration reaction, easily discouraged or frustrated

For more help, see the pages noted here:
Lying, page 92
Separation, pages 95–97
Sleep, getting to, page 98

Frustration reaction, persists

✤ **Stubbornness.** These children keep working for what they want, in spite of difficulties. As they get older, particularly when they are in school and as adults, this is a very useful trait. In the meantime, they can make your life at home challenging. When you say, "No cookie before dinner," they may bargain for half a cookie or a quarter or "at least a tiny crumb." When you say, "Stop climbing the fence," they may wait until you look the other way and then try again. They try to push past or around you. Set reasonable limits and stick to them calmly, firmly, and consistently.

Intensity of emotions, dramatic

✤ **Friends.** Intense children do better in smaller, low-energy groups. Like gasoline poured on a barbecue, large groups of intense children or adults get these children all wound up. Small groups offer more predictability and control, though *group energy* is more important than size. Invite just one preschooler over to play rather than two or three. Consider a small home daycare with six children rather than a center with twenty-five.

✤ **Sleep.** It can take intense children some time to relax, especially after a bath or even after changing into pajamas. Plan accordingly. A calm, soothing parent lowers intensity. The same familiar stories and calming music build a bridge to sleep. Around eighteen months, these youngsters often protest going to sleep. Use a baby gate if needed to keep them in their room. If you calmly and firmly hold the line, they usually adjust fairly quickly to going to sleep on their own.

For more help, see the pages noted here:
Biting and Hitting, pages 68-69, 73
Child care/Preschool, pages 67-68
Discipline, pages 70-71

Intensity, mellow

❖ **Lost in the crowd.** The mellow feelings of these children are not obvious from the outside. Take time regularly to ask and talk about their feelings. Teach them words to express their feelings.

Regularity, irregular

❖ **Discipline.** Children who have irregular bodies get tired and hungry at unexpected times. Fussing, tantrums, and difficulty following routines and rules are all worse when children are tired or hungry. Keep snacks available. Be sure they get the rest they need.

❖ **Eating.** These children may eat a lot at one meal and not much at the next. If they are hungry at 5 p.m., but not given food, their livers will release stored sugar to keep them going. So at the 6 p.m. dinnertime, they may not be hungry. The solution is to offer small nutritious snacks as they need them.

❖ **Sleep.** If this child is irregular but adapts easily, pay attention to the *child,* not the *clock* to determine bedtime. Put her down when her eyes droop. But if she is slow to adapt, a regular, scheduled bedtime routine is essential. Your job is to go through the routine at the regular time. Her job is to fall asleep when she's tired. Provide books or soothing tapes to help her pass the time in bed until she falls asleep.

❖ **Toilet training.** Irregular eating leads to irregular bowel movements. Don't plan on poops at 10 a.m. each morning.

Regularity, predictable

❖ **Time changes.** This child's body runs on its own clock. Expect her to get tired and hungry at the same time everyday, including days when your schedule is different (weekend, holidays, crisis days). It takes her longer than other people to adjust to changes in daylight saving time.

Sensitivity, high

❖ **Dependence**. Sensitive babies, of average energy level, are often content to let parents give them more help than they really need around nine to ten months of age. Thus they may appear more capable with a baby sitter than with Mom and Dad. Give your baby some time to try things for herself before you jump in to help.

❖ **Strong sensory reactions**. These children are genuinely super sensitive to their environments. Parents need to respect this trait even when they do not share it and find it hard to understand. Such children may react strongly to smells and flavors of foods, textures of clothing, temperatures, certain sounds, and light. A few of these babies have extremely sensitive skin. Being gently stroked can feel startling and unpleasant instead of soothing. Hold such a baby with gentle firmness. Think of giving gentle pressure to the muscles *under* the skin, rather than stroking the skin. As these children grow, help them accept and take care of the special needs of their bodies.

Sensitivity, low

❖ **Emotional awareness**. By age three and four years, more sensitive children automatically read other people's emotional cues and body language. Help your less sensitive preschooler learn the language of emotions. Watch videos without the sound on and talk about the feelings portrayed. Make faces at each other in the mirror and name the feelings you express. Look at the pictures in books, magazines, and newspapers together and talk about what people are feeling.

❖ **Illness**. Children with low sensitivity may be less aware of body sensations, like the pain of a beginning ear infection or a sore throat. If they are also low in intensity, they tend not to complain. If your child is listless, or out of sorts, or sleeping poorly, or eating less than usual, check for fever or other signs of illness.

❖ **Toilet training**. These children may not notice feelings inside their bodies, so they don't notice the need to use the potty. They don't notice wet or messy diapers, either. Not surprisingly, they often learn to use the potty later than other children. It is important for parents not to stress out over such normal, but later, toilet training.

Camber Chameleon

The Low Energy, Highly Adaptable Child

Like the amazing chameleon that changes its appearance to match the surroundings, Camber Chameleon blends in so well that it's hard to see him. Camber is a quiet child. While others run and yell, he plays peacefully in the sandbox. He draws, does puzzles, and builds with blocks. Camber is a parent's delight—mellow, flexible, and easy to get along with. Dinner isn't ready? He waits patiently. Dad's on the phone? He plays by himself. When his favorite bowl needs washing or his friend can't come to play, Camber is content with another bowl and is happy to play with a different friend. Camber naturally goes with the flow.

His parents attend to the squeaky wheels in their lives—hectic job, sick grandparent, Camber's difficult sister, a neighbor in need, or whatever else is happening. They have come to expect that Camber is fine and doing well. Some days, they give Camber just a quick passing smile. He doesn't complain. But if he is passed over too often he may gradually come to feel alone in a busy world. When he sees how worried his parents are, he may not bother them with his problems. In this way, he may take better care of his family than he does of himself. He can become a "little adult." Camber is at risk of losing himself in the lives of others.

Child shows: Activity, low and Adaptability, high

Keys to Living with the Quiet, Highly Adaptable Child

✦ **Check in with this child regularly.** Ask, "How are you doing? How are you feeling? Is there anything you need? What do you think about . . ." If you, the parent, are intense or high in energy, sit down, slow down, and take slow, deep breaths while you *wait* for your child's answers. Give him time to express himself.

Parent Care

You don't need to protect or replenish yourself due to constant daily demands from Camber. As the parent of a usually cooperative and responsive child, your parent-care task is different from many other parents. You get to look ahead to the long haul. Set yourself up now so that when you look back in fifteen years you'll be pleased with the choices you made when Camber was young. Heed the still, small voice in your head that knows whether or not Camber is getting what he needs from you now. This flexible child isn't likely to protest if he's getting short-changed in your time and attention. Now is the time to build a strong relationship.

Learning Style

Teachers love a whole class of Cambers. It is effortless for him to please the teacher: he just naturally adapts to most anything she offers that day. Because of low energy, he'll concentrate more on fine motor skills like art and building with small blocks than on running and jumping. He's easy to keep occupied even on rainy days. And Camber readily cooperates with the other children. His adaptability will lead him to learn a variety of things in different ways. However, just as he can get overlooked in a busy household, he can easily get overlooked in a bustling classroom. Ask him what he likes most and least. Watch to see that his personal needs are met.

Common Behavior Issues

❖ **Assertiveness, lack of.** Camber is less assertive than many other children. He doesn't feel a need to be in control because he adapts so naturally. At toddler play group, others grabbed toys out of Camber's hand. At first, Mom got angry at the other children. Then she coached Camber at home to hold on and say, "My toy." They practiced the "Holding Game" together. In preschool, several more active boys would purposely bump into Camber or his projects. Dad coached Camber to say, in a loud, strong voice, "Leave me alone!" The teacher would then come over to help. Soon the boys stopped bothering Camber.

❖ **Friends.** One of Camber's best friends is quiet and flexible like himself. They get along really well together. Camber also has a friend named Tiganda Tiger. Camber likes her and doesn't mind that Tiganda bosses him around. But Camber's mom doesn't like this behavior. So she arranged for Tiganda and Camber to take art classes together. They both liked art, and Tiganda wasn't in charge of the class! In kindergarten, Camber sometimes wants to do things *his* way. He practiced using his strong voice with Mom and Dad, so that he could tell Tiganda what he wanted.

 ## Words to Help Your Highly Flexible Child

Parent	Child
If you lovingly tell your child:	Your child learns to say:
You have needs and wishes, too.	*I have needs and wishes, too.*
What would you like to do?	*I would like to . . .*

Tarita Turtle
The Low Energy, Easily Discouraged Child

Quiet Tarita Turtle can sit so still inside her shell that one may not notice her at first. Then she proudly stretches her neck and steps out into the world. The moment things don't feel right, she quickly retreats. In Tarita's case, she retreats when she encounters difficult tasks and discouragement. When things don't work for her, she pulls back, then quietly goes off to try something else. Because she drops difficult tasks (like getting dressed) and moves on to easier ones (like playing with her toys) she can appear forgetful and disobedient. She needs help more often than other more persistent, less easily frustrated children. Therefore, she appears clingy and fragile.

Her natural motto is, "Life is too hard." Her parents must work to teach her a more useful motto: "What is an easier way to do this?" In today's busy and complex world, it's good that someone is looking for easier ways to do things! Because Tarita prefers company in case the going gets rough, she is a natural "team player."

Tarita needs positive ways to handle frustration. Her parents show her, repeatedly, how to take a more positive view of problem solving. They patiently teach her skills to deal with frustration that will last a lifetime.

Child shows: Activity, low and Frustration reaction, easily discouraged or frustrated

Keys to Living with the Quiet, Easily Discouraged Child

✤ **Break tasks into small, easy parts.** Tell her, "First put your foot through the big hole of your pants, then put your foot through the little hole." When she reaches age three or four, ask her, "How can we break this job into little parts?" Teach her this more effective way to think.

✤ **Offer frequent encouragement.** *Praise effort, not just results:* "I see you're really working hard at that," or, "Good! You're going to go back to try again." Praise partial success: "Look! We've picked up all the toys in this corner of the room."

✤ **Plan ways to work around frustration.** Tarita stops when she is too frustrated. You will have to serve up frustration in small, manageable pieces. Plan out the *number of frustrating things you fit into each day.* Allow her some choice in how much frustration she takes on: "Do you want to wear diapers or big girl pants today?" Do frustrating tasks when she is at her best, probably in the morning. Be sure she gets a good night's sleep.

✤ **Share tasks.** Tarita is a team player. Work with this natural tendency. When she reaches age three or four, make agreements with her about what she will do and what you will do: "Kitty needs food and water. Which do you want to give him? I'll do the other part."

✤ **Teach her how to ask for help.** "You're hurting the baby. When you're bored or need help or attention, tell me with words." Encourage her to say what she *can* do and then ask for the exact help she needs: "I can cut paper with my scissors, but not this cardboard." She will feel more capable and other people will be more willing to help her.

 **Parent Care**

❖ **Expect this child to complain!** Tarita Turtle is often discouraged. Life feels harder for her than for other children. She whines more than others, even with the best of parenting, because it is a learned way to get adult help. Demonstrate strong and whiny voices. Encourage her to use a strong voice.

❖ **Follow through on discipline.** Give yourself a gold star when you hold the line despite Tarita's protests.

❖ **Keep your afternoons and evenings predictable.** Stick with easy routines. As the day wears on, Tarita gets emotionally worn out. She's less able to entertain herself or deal with frustrations. She'll act up more on returning home tired than she did earlier at school. Quiet Tarita likes to snuggle with Mom and then watch a video while Mom fixes dinner.

❖ **Plan for activities.** Play groups and day care will give you some relief. Provide easy activities for the afternoon and evening: books and crayons, Legos®, easy puzzles, dolls, cars, stuffed and small plastic animals. Avoid video games or crafts that are too frustrating.

Learning Style

❙ **Child care/Preschool.** In Tarita's first preschool, there were many active children. Tarita couldn't move out of their way fast enough. Sometimes they accidentally crashed into her. Tarita felt frightened and very unhappy. She didn't know how to tell her mommy about it, so she just cried and cried. Her teachers suggested they try a different preschool. Mom found a small home day care with just five other children. There was plenty of room for the two lively children. Tarita especially liked playing with one quiet friend. She also liked being able to go from place to place and play with whatever she wanted.

❖ **Individual pace.** When she needs to learn a specific skill, it's important that she work at her own pace. She needs to feel successful at the first step before moving on to the second. No one learns well when feeling anxious. Frustration makes Tarita anxious—especially when she's alone. She learns better when a helpful parent, teacher, or fellow student is nearby to help when needed. If left alone with frustration, she simply doesn't learn.

❖ **Small muscle skills.** Because Tarita has a low activity level, she's more attracted to small muscle skills like drawing, than to big muscle skills like playing ball. Because she often sits and learns with her eyes, she may suddenly start some brand new skill that she has learned from watching others. For Tarita, practicing is frustrating and no fun, so she seldom learns for the sheer joy of mastery. When anything becomes difficult, she naturally moves on to something she can master more easily. Tarita learns best when effort quickly brings something she personally wants.

 Common Behavior Issues

❖ **Dawdling.** Left by herself, Tarita doesn't get much done. There are two reasons: Tarita doesn't have as much "natural energy" as other children for hopping around and picking up toys. Second, when any task looks difficult she quickly gets discouraged.

When Tarita went to get dressed, she'd get stuck getting her shirt or shoes on. Then she'd drift into playing with toys. When Mom told her to go clean her room, she wanted to cooperate. But when she got there, there were *too many* toys to pick up. She felt so discouraged. She'd start looking at books instead. When Mom came in, she'd demand, "Tarita, why haven't you picked up these toys? Don't you remember what you came in here for?" Mom got upset because she always had to remind Tarita. She didn't like being a nag. When Mom got angry, Tarita felt even more discouraged.

The same thing happened with brushing her teeth and feeding the cat. Everyone else thought those jobs were easy. But they were hard for Tarita. When she whined, "It's too hard," Mom answered, "No, it isn't. Just go do it!" So instead, Tarita began to say, "I didn't hear you," or, "I haven't had time yet," or, "I forgot." Mom would get angry and answer, "Tarita, why don't you ever listen?!"

Once Mom and Dad learned about temperament, they planned things differently. They understood that Tarita wasn't trying to be difficult. Until she's really comfortable, she *needs* someone nearby. She's more relaxed and more *able* to work when she has company. So Tarita brought her clothes to Mom's room, and they got dressed *together*. After a *lot* of practice, getting dressed became easy. Then Tarita started dressing in her own room. Sometimes she needed to change clothes in the late afternoon when she was tired. Then it worked better to dress with Mom nearby. Dad no longer expected Tarita to do chores by herself. Instead, they worked as a team. On Saturdays, the clean-up team works in Tarita's room early in the morning, before she gets tired. They start with, "It's time to do this together." Then they cut big jobs into little parts: first, they pick up toys in one corner, or first the animals. They make up funny songs while cleaning up to make the job more fun.

✦ **Dependence.** Because Tarita gets frustrated so easily, it takes her a long time to get comfortable doing things all by herself. Without being aware of it, Tarita gradually learned, "If I drag my feet long enough, Mom or Dad will do things for me." Waiting for Mom became her main way of handling frustration. The solution was teamwork and breaking things into small parts.

✦ **Loss.** When Tarita's Uncle Len died, Tarita was sad and discouraged. She wanted to see Uncle Len, just as she always had. The more discouraged she became, the more she seemed to forget how to do the things she had been able to do just a week before. For a while, she depended more than usual on Mom and Dad for help. With time, she became more independent again.

✦ **Shyness.** Because Tarita is low in energy, she doesn't jump into active games with the other children. She looks for friends who will help her when she needs it and not make fun of her. She makes good friends. It just takes her a while to find them.

✦ **Sleep**. It's frustrating for anyone to lie awake, waiting for sleep to come. The longer children like Tarita Turtle or her friend BeiLing Bluebird lie awake and alone, the more frustrated they get. Sometimes their bodies get so tense that they *can't* fall asleep. Children who are easily frustrated normally want company while falling asleep. They're more dependent at the end of the day. And they naturally want a parent around now, as in all other frustrating times. To stay calmer, parents remind themselves, "It's not her fault that she has trouble falling asleep. It will get easier as she grows older."

✦ *Four ways to deal with children who don't want to sleep alone.* Tarita's mom snuggled with her in her room for half an hour until Tarita fell asleep. She became Tarita's bridge into sleep. Not surprisingly, Tarita had great difficulty falling asleep when Mom was out for the evening. When Tarita turned three, Mom said, "I'll snuggle with you for ten minutes. Then I will stay nearby if you don't talk." Mom read, meditated, or did her exercises on the floor. When Tarita turned four, she gradually found she could fall asleep by herself.

BeiLing's favorite place to sleep was in Mom and Dad's bed. But he wiggled and kicked so much that they couldn't sleep, so they play musical beds. BeiLing wanted Mom near him while he fell asleep. Mom often fell asleep before BeiLing did. Then Mom woke up and went to sleep with Dad. After a while, BeiLing would come to their bed. Dad woke up and felt too crowded, so he went to sleep in BeiLing's room. Eventually, BeiLing learned to fall asleep in his own room without Mom. Then his parents bought a larger bed, so they could all sleep together after BeiLing joined them at 4 a.m.

Next door, his cousin BeiShu also liked to sleep in her parents' bed. But because she's so sensitive, she woke whenever her mother moved, so BeiShu's parents didn't let her sleep in their bed. She slept on a blanket *beside* their bed. Over the course of several months, her parents gradually moved the blanket farther from their bed, then gradually down the hall to her own room. On rare occasions, she needed a reassuring word or pat.

Down the block, Kapper's parents wanted him to sleep by himself in his own room. It was especially difficult during the toddler years. Kapper cried, but got himself to sleep. Then he got an ear infection. Bedtime crying started over again. Mom gave reassuring pats, but held the line as soon as his ear was better. They made sure he had reminders of Mom and Dad. When he turned two, they put their picture on the wall and played a tape of their voices singing his favorite songs. Mom encouraged his progress, "You're able to go to sleep by yourself!" Kapper protested from time to time, but Mom was sure Kapper could manage. When he turned three, Dad helped him plan quiet things to think about while falling asleep—a cloud floating in the sky or a spaceship sliding past stars.

✦ **Stubbornness.** Tarita's Aunt Trina complained that Tarita was stubborn. She didn't know that for children like Tarita, stubbornness is made, not born. She expected Tarita to do many things she wasn't able to do, *especially* by herself. She expected her to dress herself, to hold her spoon the right way, and to practice longer at new games. Everything at Aunt Trina's house was too hard! If Tarita said, "I can't do that," Aunt Trina answered, "Yes, you can! Just try. Don't be a quitter!" Tarita felt discouraged. She accidentally discovered if she said, "I *won't* do it," Aunt Trina acted differently. She didn't say, "You can do it. Just try." Instead, she stood silently and glared at Tarita. Sometimes she called Mom to come early to get Tarita. Tarita and Aunt Trina never got along well. Sadly, Aunt Trina never understood why.

✦ **Testing limits; temper tantrums.** Tarita Turtle doesn't like rules. Rules are frustrating! Frustration sometimes leads to tantrums. She often attacks the limit to see if it will go away. She wasn't allowed to pour juice on the floor yesterday or the day before or the day before that. But, is it okay today?

Before Mom learned about temperament, she expected Tarita to play all by herself. But playing is discouraging! Blocks tumble down. Puzzle pieces don't fit. Crayons break. Tarita wanted someone nearby, to help out. Over time, she discovered it was easier to throw a block— and get Mom's attention!—than to get one block to stack on top of another.

Around eighteen months Tarita discovered an easy way to get Dad's attention. (Remember, Tarita is always looking for an easy way!) She grinned and pushed the VCR buttons *again*. Dad tried to be patient, but Tarita pushed the buttons faster and harder. Eventually, Dad realized Tarita's goal was not to play with the VCR, but to get attention. Trying to please Tarita by being patient didn't help. So instead, Dad firmly said, "Tarita, you can't be in the family room if you touch the VCR. You must go to your room until you can come out and not touch the VCR." He carried her to her room three times daily for a week until Tarita learned. (Other children may need slightly longer or shorter room restrictions and may learn after more or fewer times.)

Gradually, Mom and Dad accepted the fact that Tarita couldn't play by herself as long as other children. So they took turns spending time with her. They also arranged exchanges with other families, so sometimes they watched several children together, and at other times, they had time off.

✦ **Weaning.** Tarita weaned more slowly than active youngsters who prefer to be on the move with bottle or cup in hand. Tarita liked to cuddle with Mom. She wasn't in a hurry to go anywhere! To avoid frustration, Mom waited until Tarita could drink easily from a cup. Then she cut the morning nursing first. That's when Tarita could most easily handle frustration.

Words to Help Your Child Live with Frustration

Parent

If you lovingly tell your child:

How can we break this into smaller, easier parts?

Everyone needs to practice.

This will get easier with practice.

Let's take a short break and come back to this.

You'll know when you're ready to do this by yourself.

What part can you do? And what part do you need help with?

Everyone gets frustrated. It's what you do next that counts.

Child

Your child learns to say:

How can I break this into smaller, easier parts?

Everyone needs to practice.

This will get easier with practice.

I'll take a short break and come back to this.

I'll know when I'm ready to do this by myself.

I can do . . . I need help with . . .

Everyone gets frustrated. It's what I do next that counts.

Tarita Turtle shares these behavior issues with other children profiled in this book. For more help, see the pages noted here:

Child care/Preschool, pp. 86-87

Self-esteem, low, pp. 93-95

Separation, pp. 95-97

Sibling rivalry, pp. 97-98

Sleep, pp. 57-58, 75-76, 98-100

Testing limits, temper tantrums, pp. 100-101, 109

Toilet training, pp. 101

Fenler Fawn
The Sensitive, Intense, Cautious Child

Fenler Fawn is naturally sensitive and cautious. Only when conditions are exactly right does he stand up and step into the clearing in the woods. No amount of coaxing or yelling brings him out sooner. When he feels cautious, he feels very, very cautious. Because he is intense, *all* of his feelings are strong.

Fenler practices new things in his head long before he practices with his body. Although it takes him longer to get started, with time he becomes as comfortable and confident as other children his age. Fenler becomes anxious if pushed into situations before he is ready. Adrenaline, the fight or flight hormone, pours into his blood stream. His heart pounds and his hands get sweaty. He feels truly afraid. Then his body freezes up, just like any other fawn that hides by lying perfectly still. It isn't so much that he *will* not move, but that he *cannot* move.

In new situations, Fenler *looks* before he leaps. He *enjoys* watching and learns a great deal that way. He stood at the sidelines of his best friend's birthday party. Afterwards, he told Aunt Brenda all about it with as much pleasure as if he had played the games and tasted all the treats himself.

Child shows: Sensitivity, high; Intensity, high; and Approach, cautious

Keys to Living with the Sensitive, Intense, Cautious Child

❖ **Divide new tasks into small steps.** Fenler needs to practice new things step by step. For several weeks, Fenler climbed up and down the stairs of the slide, without once sliding down. This is how his internal sense of security grows. With each practiced step, he learns what comes next. The more familiar the event, the more secure he feels.

❖ **Expect caution in all that is new.** Fenler's parents now expect him to resist all that is new. So Dad gives him time to watch and practice in his head before joining in. At the park, they watched other children on the slide. "Would you like to slide?" asked Dad. "No!" answered Fenler. So Dad took him each day to *watch* the other children. While Dad waited, he told himself, "In time, Fenler will be ready."

Grandpa gets frustrated with how long it takes Fenler to start new things. Grandpa tries to push Fenler into new situations before he is ready. But Mom says, "No, if we push him too fast, he will become more and more afraid of new situations. People don't like to feel *really* frightened. For Fenler, it's better to move slowly into new situations. When he goes at his own speed, his body can relax. Then he gradually learns to feel more comfortable when facing new things."

❖ **Help Fenler *feel* comfortable.** Remember walking with a rock in your shoe? Fenler may feel the same about the tag in his shirt. Cut the tags out of his clothes and don't make him wear what he tells you is uncomfortable. A comfortable body calms the mind. Over time, help Fenler take care of his own sensitive body.

❖ **Provide relaxed companionship in new situations.** When Fenler was ready, Dad held him tight and they slid down the slide together. Fenler held on for dear life! After several more weeks, Fenler wanted to try all by himself. If his parents always took his first "No!" as the final answer, Fenler's life would remain very narrow. As he grew older, Fenler was fine with a teacher or a friend to keep him company in new situations.

Parent Care

In a society which glorifies assertiveness and independence, you're likely to get a lot of critical glances. Those who don't understand temperament will believe your over-indulgence created Fenler's caution. Know in your heart that this sensitive being arrived on your doorstep with his own inborn temperament. You are creating a safe, comfortable environment in which he can grow and flourish.

Learning Style

❖ **Child care/Preschool.** Like other cautious children, Fenler does best in a program with structure and consistency. Then there aren't too many new things at once. His teacher tells the children ahead of time what is going to happen. Having older children around gives Fenler a chance to watch new things before he tries them.

When Fenler started his new preschool, Dad stayed with him longer than the other parents needed to stay with their children. For many days Fenler sat on the side and watched. It looked like he wasn't doing anything at all. But in his mind, he was practicing the activities and the school routine. Neither Dad nor his teachers pushed him. They invited him, but let him go at his own pace. When he was ready, he joined in.

Mom has learned that when Fenler gets all the sleep he needs and snacks when he is hungry, he has more emotional energy to cope with new things that come along each day. She keeps afternoons and evenings as routine as possible. Late in the day, Fenler is less able to handle new routines or experiences.

Fenler learns with his eyes. Teachers call him a "visual learner." At preschool, he watched everyday for a week as a classmate put a puzzle together. The next week, Fenler easily put it together by himself.

Common Behavior Issues

❖ **Activities and lessons.** Before signing up for a series of lessons (such as swimming, art, or music), Mom first takes Fenler to watch. Then, when Fenler is ready to join in, Mom enrolls him in the program.

✦ **Biting.** Fenler has strong feelings all through his body, even in his mouth. When he was little, he sometimes gave Mom a hug and a happy bite on the shoulder. Mom set Fenler down immediately, left the room, and counted slowly to ten. Mom did the same thing when Fenler bit out of anger.

When Fenler bit a playmate, Mom picked him up, and said firmly, "Don't bite people. Biting hurts." She moved Fenler away for a minute or two. Mom gave him rubber toys to bite. As Fenler neared two, Mom said, "Let's play the angry game." Mom then clenched her teeth and growled. Fenler gradually learned new things to do with an angry mouth.

At age three, Fenler started a new preschool. The teacher reported that Fenler had bitten several children. Mom explained that Fenler gets overwhelmed when too many children crowd too close. So the teacher showed Fenler a quiet corner where he could go to be by himself when he needed more space. She also taught Fenler to hold out his arm and say, "Stop, I need this much space." Once he had a way to protect his space, Fenler stopped biting other children.

✦ **Danger.** Mom knew Fenler would need time to get comfortable at the new swimming pool. So she took a magazine to fill her waiting time. As usual in new situations, Fenler hung back in fear, watching others splash and swim. After he'd become comfortable, he approached the pool. Knowing that everyone learns better when they are relaxed, Mom now came to Fenler and told him the new safety rules: "Don't run near the pool. Never go in the pool alone." Fenler objected to the rules. Mom calmly told him the rules again on several occasions. She reminded herself that Fenler was objecting to the *newness* of the rules, not necessarily the rules themselves.

✦ **Eating.** Fenler likes to stick to favorite foods. When he was a baby, he wrinkled his nose and pushed out all new foods with his busy little tongue. Dad knew to offer a tiny taste of the same food a number of times. Often, by the third or fifth time, Fenler realized he liked apricots or applesauce. However, he never liked new foods when he was really hungry or tired. As a preschooler, he would eat mashed carrots, but scream at carrot pieces in soup. They seemed too different! His sensitive body has to take in so many new things that he needs his food to be just the same from one time to the next.

Fenler eats only a few foods. Mom loves all kinds of interesting, different foods. But she knows Fenler has his own way with food, and it's important not to get in fights about what he eats. She knows that combining milk or cheese or beans with wheat or rice gives Fenler as much protein as meat. Because he eats so few fruits or vegetables, she also gives him a daily vitamin so that he gets the nutrition he needs. At age five, he still doesn't eat nearly as many different foods as his adventuresome cousin. But sometimes at a party or picnic, he'll try a new food after watching other children eat it.

✦ **New events.** Many ordinary, but new events frighten Fenler Fawn. Even a phone call from Grandma can frighten him. At first, when she called, he just listened on the phone. Grandma said, "Hello, Fenler! How are you?" To help, Dad started asking Fenler, "What do you want to tell Grandma when you talk?' Then Fenler could practice, "Hi, Grandma. I go watch swimming lessons with Mommy." Finally he was ready for the real thing, and Grandma was delighted.

Before the family traveled to visit Uncle Tad in Tennessee, they visited the airport and read books about airplanes. They talked about exactly what would happen—the check-in counter, the meals, and the bathroom. Then they played "travel." They packed his suitcase and lined up chairs like airplane seats. For a week, Fenler practiced sleeping in the sleeping bag he would take. They practiced saying hello and goodbye. Mom talked of where everyone would sleep, what the schedule might be, and sights they would see. They looked at lots of pictures of Uncle Tad and his family. Mom also called Uncle Tad before they arrived, and reminded him that Fenler might need some distance at first. Fenler would be ready for hugs and kisses after he'd had a day or two to warm up. All the preparation took time and effort. However, it was worth it. The whole family enjoyed the trip. Because many things were familiar, Fenler relaxed and had fun, too.

✦ **Separation.** Fenler Fawn is less upset about Mom leaving the house than he is about having a new sitter. So Mom asks a new sitter to come by a couple times to get acquainted, so Fenler doesn't feel alone with a stranger. When he was little, Mom first left him for only fifteen or twenty minutes at a time. Once he was used to the sitter, she left him for longer periods. When possible, Mom found sitters who could come to their house, rather than taking Fenler to the sitter's house. That way, Fenler didn't have to get used to a new sitter *and* a new house.

✦ **Sleep.** When Fenler was a baby, he cried harder when Mom walked in his room and picked him up! Sensitive youngsters often feel surprised and upset when their personal space is *suddenly* invaded. Mom learned to stand nearby and sing or talk for a moment. Then she would stroke him, and finally pick him up. Some months later, mornings were difficult because Mom had to wake Fenler before he was ready. Over the next of several weeks, Dad moved bedtime a few minutes earlier each night. Then, Fenler was able to wake up slowly on his own. Fenler's day started off much better. He still gets upset if he wakes up suddenly, or if someone wakes him. But now, at age six, he understands. His parents have often told him, "You woke up too fast. You feel better if you wake up slowly."

Fenler's cousin, who is also sensitive and intense, cried briefly in the morning for several months. Life was going fairly smoothly. She just needed to let off tension by crying before she could face the day. Her mom stayed calm and soothing, and finally the phase passed.

✦ *Falling asleep.* With a sensitive body and strong emotions, it is often hard for Fenler to fall asleep. Mom and Dad have learned to use the same bedtime routine, because Fenler doesn't take to new things at the end of the day. His parents help Fenler relax and get comfortable. When he was a baby, his parents used a warm bath and quiet music. As he got older, he liked to take a walk with Dad, then listen to stories or sing. Now he likes to color quietly before the story. Once he's in bed, he likes a back rub while he talks about his day. Not surprisingly, Fenler has more trouble falling asleep when he's getting used to something new, like sleeping in a new room or starting a new school. Since age four, there's always been an imaginary "worry envelope" beside his bed, so any worries at bedtime could be "put away in the worry envelope" until morning.

When Fenler turned twenty months old, his parents decided it was time to set a fixed bedtime each night and not stay with him until he fell asleep. They put a baby gate at the doorway, so he couldn't leave his room. They expected it to take a toddler like Fenler a few weeks to get used to a new routine. Because of his intensity, they also expected Fenler would cry long and hard. Mom didn't think she could stand listening to him cry and protest. She decided to go for a walk. After Dad put Fenler in his room, he was determined to ignore the protest, which lasted about twenty minutes each night for two weeks. When Fenler knew the new routine and knew it wouldn't change, he stopped crying each night when Dad left the room.

✦ **Stress.** Given his strong feelings and the time he needs to get used to new things, it's not surprising that Fenler is upset by life's big changes. His emotional stress often shows up in backsliding. When under stress, he's often unable to do things he could do before. After moving to a new house, Fenler kept having potty accidents, so his parents put him back in diapers for six weeks. For a month after starting a new preschool, Fenler seemed unable to feed himself breakfast or get dressed by himself. For three weeks after Grandpa died, he couldn't remember his job of feeding the cat. Family illness, divorce, and other such stress usually bring a similar reaction to children of this temperament.

As he got older, Fenler asked *lots* of questions about new things that worried him. He asked some questions again and again. Even after Fenler's parents gave good, clear answers, he still asked the same questions repeatedly. His parents felt frustrated, but they realized he needed time and repetition to make sense of new things. He needed to update the pictures in his mind about how his life works. "Why did Grandpa die? Is heaven in the ground, where they put him?" Dad listened patiently and talked with Fenler about his feelings and his worries. Dad said, "People die when they get very old or very sick. Mom and I are not old and not sick, so we will be here to take care of you. I miss Grandpa a lot. I feel sad. Do you feel sad, too, Fenler?"

Mom knew Fenler would have to work with this big, new issue for a long time. She found some books at the library about death, which Fenler wanted to read again and again. Each afternoon as they came in from the garage, they stopped to bury a leaf or flower in the garden. They talked about the new plants that would grow. Some days Mom was tired and rushed. She had little patience to stop to bury *another* leaf. But she could also see that repeating this ritual again and again helped Fenler gradually to understand the mysteries of life.

✦ **Testing limits.** Because he doesn't like new things, Fenler Fawn needs time to get used to new rules and routines. As much as possible, Mom and Dad tell him about new rules ahead of time: "We are getting a new living room carpet tomorrow. After that, we can only eat at the table." Fenler always complains that new rules aren't fair, but Mom just repeats the rule calmly. After the new carpet arrived, he needed more calm, clear reminding. Dad knew he wasn't trying to be disobedient. It just takes Fenler time to get into a new routine. For a week, Mom consistently reminded him: "Fenler, we don't want spills on the new carpet. Where do we have to eat now?" When Fenler complained and wouldn't go to the table, Dad calmly picked up his plate and took it back to the table. Unfortunately, some grape juice spilled on the carpet. Thinking back, Mom realized it would have been better to change the eating rule a week *before* the new carpet arrived.

✦ **Toilet training.** Like everything else, Fenler was slow to take to potty training. As usual, his parents broke potty training into parts. Watching was the first step—watching Mom and Dad and watching other children in daycare. (When his cousins visited, Mom asked them if Fenler could go in and watch.) One by one, as he became interested, Fenler practiced each little step—flushing the toilet, getting toilet paper, getting his clothes on and off, saying when he was about to wet a diaper, wiping his bottom, and sitting on the potty. Once he'd learned all the parts, he was ready to put it all together. One morning he announced, "I don't wear diapers anymore!" Mom was glad she hadn't spent time and energy pushing, because in fact, when he was ready, he was ready.

Words to Help Your Child Live with a Cautious Nature

Parent	Child
If you lovingly tell your child:	Your child learns to say:
You don't like surprises.	*I don't like surprises.*
You like to know what's coming.	*I like to know what's coming.*
You need time to get used to new things.	*I need time to get used to new things.*
You can practice in your mind to get ready.	*I can practice in my mind to get ready.*
You know when you are ready.	*I know when I am ready.*
Tell me when you are ready.	*I'll tell you when I am ready.*

Words to Help Your Child Live with High Sensitivity

Parent	Child
If you lovingly tell your child:	Your child learns to say:
You notice things that other people don't.	*I notice things that other people don't.*
Many people aren't bothered by noise, movement, or strong feelings all around them. You're learning to take a break when you need one, so you can feel calm again.	*Other people aren't bothered by noise, movement, or feeling all around them. I'm learning to take a break when I need one, so I can feel calm again.*
How can we make your body feel better?	*How can I make my body feel better?*
You are good at noticing how other people feel.	*I am good at noticing how other people feel.*

Words to Help Your Child Live with High Intensity

Parent	Child
If you lovingly tell your child:	Your child learns to say:
You have big, strong feelings.	*I have big strong feelings.*
Your feelings are strong and fast like racing horses.	*My feelings are strong and fast like racing horses.*
How fast are your horses running right now?	*How fast are my horses running right now?*
What can calm your horses now?	*What can calm my horses now?*
You're learning to control your racing horses.	*I'm learning to control my racing horses.*
You can think and plan better when your horses are resting.	*I can think and plan better when my horses are resting.*

Tiganda Tiger
The Intense, Slow-Adapting Child

There are no minor events in the life of Tiganda Tiger. All her feelings are big. She is either rolling in delight or roaring in anger. As a small child, her intensity rose faster than her words could come out, so she bit and hit instead.

Tiganda is intense *and* slow to adapt. Transitions and changes are hard for her. The higher her intensity, the harder it is to change her course. She becomes a high-powered engine caught on a circular track. Even transitions she's made hundreds of times before are hard—waking up, setting aside a toy before lunch, getting into the car. People who don't understand temperament call her bossy and stubborn. But refusing to go with the flow is her way of saying, "Wait! I can't change that fast!" Tiganda doesn't have to remain a resister. With help, she becomes a natural planner.

Child shows: Intensity, dramatic and Adaptability, low

🐘 Keys to Living with the Intense, Slow-adapting Child

✤ **Adaptation energy, small tank of.** Cars have different-sized tanks of gas or energy. Small tanks need to be refilled more often. Similarly, it takes energy to make changes. And some people are born with smaller tanks of "adaptation energy." Tiganda has a very small tank. She instinctively rations the little bit of adaptation energy she has. She demands to wear a skirt instead of a jumper, that Mommy take her to school, and that the night light be off *after* the back rub. This saves adaptation energy for big things, like the new child in day care, a shopping trip, a substitute teacher, or Dad leaving on a business trip.

Just as the gas tank runs low toward the end of a trip, adaptation energy runs low toward the end of the day. The lower the sun is in the sky, the lower Tiganda's ability to adapt. Small unexpected events like a different route home from school because a road is closed, or an unexpected change in baby sitters, may cause a tantrum. When her adaptation energy is all gone, Tiganda may demand something just for the sake of demanding. Then, when Mom gives in, she screams for the opposite. There seems to be no way to please or calm her.

Because of Tiganda's low adaptability, her parents work hard to keep afternoons and evenings as predictable and routine as possible. Sleep fills up her tank of adaptation energy. For the day to go smoothly, she needs a good night's sleep the night before.

✤ **Avoid the intensity spiral.** Intensity fuels intensity. When Mom yells, "Stop that!" or, "Be quiet!" or spanks Tiganda for hitting another child, Tiganda's intensity rises even higher. So instead, Mom tries to lower her own intensity. She takes several deep breaths and talks in a soft, quiet voice. She keeps her hands at her sides. Mom *pretends* she is a calm newspaper reporter: "Tiganda, I can see you are really disappointed and angry that we have to leave early today," or, "You may not hit your brother. Hitting hurts." Later by herself, Mom may scream into her pillow or exercise to let off steam. But as much as possible, she *acts* calm when Tiganda is intense.

✤ **Channel intensity into forms you can live with.** Singing and drama are great outlets for intense emotions. Make up stories and plays with stuffed animals.

✦ **Expect difficulty with transitions and changes.** Everything from waking every morning to wearing a new shirt is difficult.

Talk about transitions and changes head of time. The more Tiganda knows about what is ahead, the more easily she can make the change. Before she can tell time, use an egg timer to announce changes. Turn daily events into routines that announce changes: "After breakfast, we'll get in the car and go to the park. After lunch it will be nap time. After story time at day care, Mom will come pick you up." At age three or four, use a kitchen timer to announce changes: "In five minutes, we will . . . When the big hand of the clock gets to the top, we will go." Around age four, put a one-week calendar in her room: hang seven papers on the wall, with a picture to remind her of what usually happens each day. Nothing fancy is needed. Use stick figures or symbols—a green triangle for day care, or a different-colored line when each parent is away.

✦ **Expect strong reactions.** Temper tantrums are a *routine* part of Tiganda's early years. Fortunately, yelling and tantrums are not life-threatening—even though they sound like it! If parents often back off for fear of Tiganda's strong reactions, then Tiganda's intensity rules the household. (And Tiganda will be frightened by how much people resent her.) Because she is slow to adapt, expect especially strong reactions to sudden changes. When parents stay calm and firm, these intense reactions blow over sooner. Dad says to himself, "This is just intensity. I can stay quiet and firm."

✦ **Mind pictures must change before behavior can change.** Tiganda is a natural planner. She lives with pictures in her head of what's going to happen next. Once she pictures Glenview Park, Cranbrook Park will not do. Before she can change her behavior, she needs time to change the picture in her head. At age two, Mom tells her five to ten minutes ahead of time what is going to happen next. At three, Dad tells her as much as possible about the plan for the next day. When possible, they make only a few changes at a time. Then she has time to get comfortable with one thing before adjusting to another. The more she knows about the future, the more secure and relaxed she feels inside.

✦ **Rules and rituals are relaxing!** Tiganda loves rules and rituals (once they are familiar). They help her know what happens next. Life is more predictable. There are fewer surprises. Tiganda will be happiest if she—

- eats and drinks out of the same green bowl and cup,
- puts Duck-Duck in the tub before she herself gets in,
- sits in the same place in the car,
- always takes a swish down the slide before leaving the park,
- gets three kisses before going to sleep.

As Tiganda gets older, the rituals can get more complex, such as looking out at the thermometer before putting on a coat and eating French toast every Tuesday for breakfast. When Tiganda turned four, family meetings became really important. When the family worked together to make plans and rules, there were fewer surprises.

✣ **Teeter-totter effect.** Tiganda lives on an emotional teeter-totter. When her intensity is high, her adaptability is low. Flexibility increases only as intensity comes down. Even happy occasions, like a birthday party, raise emotional intensity. Then adaptability drops. The key is learning to bring intensity down *before* it skyrockets.

Parent Care

✣ **Discount sale.** Intense children learn that intensity alone can bring adults running. Tiganda's mom finally understood that Tiganda gets upset by every little thing. She seems to exaggerate everything. So Mom learned to think like she does at a "30% off" sale. The real price, or the real problem, is 30% less than it sounds at first. Thinking this way helps Mom stay calm when Tiganda is upset. If it's not a real emergency, Mom doesn't run.

✣ **The Give-in/Get-tough cycle.** Without intending to, Tiganda's parents fall into a vicious cycle. Hoping to avoid yelling and tantrums, they give in more than they really want to. Tiganda then pushes more and more. Suddenly her parents are angry and resentful. So they get too tough and demanding. Then her parents feel guilty, give in, and the whole cycle begins again. The way out of the give-in/get-tough cycle is to calmly and firmly *hold the line sooner.* There will be mighty protest at first, but as the rules get more consistent, life becomes smoother. Consistency is the way out of the give-in/get-tough cycle.

✣ **Lack of respect.** Grandpa complained, "When you tell Tiganda to do something, she should do it! You are the parents!" Mom explained, "Tiganda isn't trying to be bad or disrespectful. She can't make fast changes. Many of us live in a 4-wheel drive vehicle that can go anywhere. Tiganda lives in a train on a track—she has to build a new track before she can go somewhere different." Over the years, Grandpa still didn't get it. Mom thought, "Maybe Grandpa is also slow to adapt!"

 ## Learning Style

❖ **Child care/Preschool.** Mom carefully picked a preschool for Tiganda. She looked for balance between planned and unplanned time. Mom knows that a regular schedule is easier for Tiganda to picture in her head. On the other hand, Tiganda needs more time than other children to change from one activity to another. She needs teachers who understand and help her with transitions. Free-floating games with other children use up a lot of adaptation energy. When she was little, Tiganda could only handle short periods of give-and-take with other children. She gets along best in small groups of children her own age, who are not especially active. Large groups get too intense. Younger children are too unpredictable. Older children and very active children overwhelm her—she simply can't adapt quickly enough to keep up with them.

At four and a half, Tiganda's behavior at home suddenly became much worse. She started misbehaving more, hitting her brother, and having tantrums about everything. Her parents were discouraged. Things were much worse than just a few months before. Mom thought it was just a phase. Dad thought they needed firmer discipline. Tiganda's teacher reported that Tiganda was terrific and seemed well adjusted. Her parents wondered what they were doing wrong.

They made an appointment with a child psychologist. Mom went to observe at school. She noticed how loud the room was. Tiganda wandered from activity to activity without really becoming involved. When she finally started a project, she needed to stop because it was time for a group activity. The psychologist suggested they try a different school—quieter, with fewer children, and where the activities were structured, but would allow Tiganda to move at her own pace. Tiganda's behavior at home improved immediately and remarkably. Tiganda had been unable to say how much stress she had felt at school. She used all her adaptation energy at school and had none left when she came home. Her new school was calm and predictable. She felt secure while playing and learning. Even though the old school was excellent, it hadn't been a good fit for Tiganda.

When Tiganda started kindergarten, she made plans with Dad, based on her temperament. At the beginning of the year, she sometimes went to the school library instead of out to recess. There, she could more easily stay calm, and there was less to adapt to than on a playground full of children. When she started going out for recess, she looked for small groups of children to play with. At lunch time, she sat at the edge of the playground to eat. There was too much going on out in the middle of it! Having these options in her head helped her feel more control over her environment and herself.

 Common Behavior Issues

✤ **Afternoons are awful.** At the end of the day, Tiganda was often upset and grouchy. By the time she got home from school, she'd used up her whole tank of adaptation energy. Mom gradually learned to plan a very regular and predictable afternoon and evening. Life then became easier for everyone.

✤ **Arguing.** When Tiganda Tiger turned four, her Aunt Sarah moved to town. Once Tiganda got to know her, she liked to visit overnight. Every time Aunt Sarah asked Tiganda to do something, like brush her teeth, Tiganda argued. She'd say, "I can't brush my teeth now because I might want a snack," or, "Teddy Bear hasn't brushed his teeth yet," or, "You're not the boss of me." Aunt Sarah found Tiganda's visits very difficult. Mom explained to Aunt Sarah: "Because Tiganda is slow to adapt, she argues while she gets ready to make a change." Aunt Sarah changed her approach. She'd say, "Tiganda, let's play 'Candyland' after dinner. We'll set the timer to play for twenty minutes. Then it will be time to brush your teeth and read one story. If you don't brush your teeth by 8:30 p.m., we won't have time to read a story." When Tiganda could see the whole plan in her mind ahead of time, she didn't argue nearly so much.

✤ **Biting.** Tiganda has strong feelings all through her body. When she was little, she sometimes gave a happy hug and bit Mom on the shoulder. She felt big feelings even in her mouth. Mom yelped, "Ouch! That hurts!" in surprise. She set Tiganda down immediately, left the room, and counted slowly to ten. Mom did the same thing when Tiganda bit out of anger.

When Tiganda bit a playmate, Mom picked her up, said firmly, "Don't bite people. Biting hurts," and moved Tiganda away for a minute or two. Mom gave her rubber toys to bite. As Tiganda neared two, Mom said, "Let's play the angry game." Mom then clenched her teeth and growled. Tiganda gradually learned something new to do with her teeth when she was angry. A neighbor advised her mom to bite Tiganda back, but Mom said, "I can't teach her that it's wrong to bite if I bite her! It's my job to show Tiganda what *to* do."

❖ **Breath holding.** One day when Tiganda was eighteen months old, Mom walked into the living room and found Tiganda happily scribbling on the wall with crayons. Mom took the crayons away. Tiganda got upset because she liked marking pretty colors on the wall. She reached out her hands and stamped her feet to tell Mom how much she wanted the crayons, but Mom wouldn't give them to her. Tiganda got so angry and her body got so tight, that she didn't breathe! Gradually, the color in her face turned from pink to grayish blue. Mom got very frightened! She called Tiganda's name and patted her, but nothing seemed to help. Finally, Tiganda started to breathe again. Mom was so relieved she burst into tears. Later that morning, Mom called the doctor. Because he knew Tiganda was in good physical health, he said, "This happens sometimes with very intense children. Even if she held her breath so long that she passed out, she would automatically start breathing again. It looks frightening, but isn't dangerous," he advised. The same thing happened several more times. Once Tiganda learned to talk well, she could say or yell what she wanted and no longer held her breath.

❖ **Danger.** Tiganda adapts slowly to new rules—even rules about danger. Not only that, but the more strongly (or intensely) the rule is stated, the harder it is for Tiganda to change her actions and follow the rule. One day Tiganda was so excited about the birthday party she had just left, that she forgot to wait at the corner for Mom to catch up. Another day Tiganda's ball rolled into the street. All Tiganda's attention was on running to get the ball. Dad shouted, "Tiganda! Stop!" When Tiganda heard her father's intense voice, she became more anxious and intense. But her higher intensity was still focused on the ball. So she ran *faster* into the street. Luckily there were no cars coming. Dad was really scared! When Tiganda feels intense, she is *less able* to refocus her mind onto something else. Both parents learned to pay special attention when Tiganda's intensity was high, or when they were near dangerous places.

Clearly, Tiganda needs reminders of rules *before* her intensity rises. She needs to practice safety rules in her mind *before* she is in danger. So they made up games like "parking lot." They set up chairs like the car, and practiced the rule: "In the parking lot, hold Dad's hand, or touch the car." Even after their game, Tiganda forgot and walked away from the car one day. Dad calmly brought her back. She had to touch the car before they started out together. Of course, Tiganda screamed while Dad held her hand against the car for a moment. To keep the rules fresh in her mind, Dad asked Tiganda about one safety rule each night before bedtime stories: "To be safe, what do you do when your ball goes into the street?" Because Tiganda was calm, it was a good time for her to practice safety rules in her head. She gradually did better and better at following safety rules during the day.

✤ **Discipline**. Early on, Mom expected Tiganda to leave her toys on a moment's notice to get in the car. When Dad said, "Move," he expected Tiganda to move! Tiganda didn't move. Her parents didn't realize that a sudden, strong "Go!" or "Stop!" *increases Tiganda's intensity and lowers her flexibility*. Then it's harder for her to cooperate, even if she wants to. Mom and Dad got frustrated and angry. Tiganda had one temper tantrum after another. Everyone was miserable.

Mom talked with other mothers. Discipline sounded easy for them. They used:

Time-outs: "Stop! You hit your brother, so go to your room!"

Take-aways: "You left your bike on the sidewalk last night so you can't ride it today."

Restrictions: "We can't go to the park until you wipe up the juice you spilled."

But these methods made things worse with Tiganda. She screamed, hit, kicked, and broke things. Tiganda's parents felt confused, discouraged, and angry.

One thinks ahead when around a tiger in the jungle. Around Tiganda, one thinks ahead to make life predictable and thereby give her enough time to make changes and transitions.

Gradually, her parents understood that Tiganda *can't* change quickly. She always needs time to change the picture in her mind before she can change her body. Tiganda resists new rules at first. But once they are part of her mind picture, she *likes* rules and routines. They make her life predictable.

Mom and Dad have learned to tell Tiganda about new rules *ahead of time,* whenever possible. The less rules surprise her, the less they upset her. (Not that she doesn't complain!) If rules change, Tiganda's day is full of surprises. Tiganda *hates* surprises. The better her expectations match the real world, the smoother her life. The more familiar the rule, the easier it is to follow. The more she knows what will happen next, the more secure and relaxed she feels.

❖ *Four ways to discipline the intense, slow-adapting child.*
Give two yeses and then a consequence. "You can pour water in the tub or splash water in the tub. If you splash water out of the tub again, your bath will be over."

Transition time. "We need to get ready to go in 10 minutes."

Set a kitchen timer for five minutes. When it rings, say, "Five more minutes."

When the timer goes off, Tiganda still grumbles and complains. But that's much better than a full-blown tantrum. When Tiganda turned four, she set the timer by herself.

Contracts. "Is it easier to pick up your toys every day before dinner or after dinner?" asked Mom. "After dinner. I'm not so hungry," Tiganda said. "What consequences should we use if you don't pick up your toys?" her mom asked. When Tiganda couldn't think of a consequence, Mom said, "Then I'll pick them up and put them away out of reach for a week." Tiganda answered, "I don't like that! How about I can't watch a video until I pick up the toys?" Mom answered, "We're talking about toys, not videos." Tiganda replied, "Then put the toys away for two days." "That's fine. We have a contract!" agreed Mom.

Contracts match Tiganda's temperament because they are planned ahead of time. After ages three, contracts became more and more useful.

Count-down rewards. Sometimes they made contracts about count-down rewards. Each morning, Mom gave Tiganda ten checkers. She didn't have to earn them. She got them because Tiganda is a terrific girl. Her mom was willing to remind her one time about the things Tiganda should not do (like hit her brother). However, if Tiganda forgot and hit him, Mom gave one reminder, then took away a checker. When Tiganda still had nine checkers at the end of the day, Mom complimented her on how hard it is to keep her hands under control and how well she had done. Tiganda likes contracts because they help her feel successful and in control. More and more often, Tiganda had all ten checkers at the end of the day. She felt very proud!

❖ **Divorce, coping with.** Tiganda's friend Skyler has the same temperament as Tiganda. After much difficulty at home, his parents divorced. They hoped Skyler would adjust quickly. But changes are hard for Skyler. It was hard to live in two different houses. It was especially hard because schedules and family rules were very different in each house. Skyler's stubbornness and tantrums showed how unhappy he was. His parents met with a therapist. She said, "Because of Skyler's temperament, he can't make so many changes. To help Skyler, *you* need to make changes so schedules and rules are more the same in both houses." Fortunately, his parents were able to set their own feelings aside enough to make compromises for Skyler. As life became more similar in both houses, Skyler felt more secure and happier.

✤ **Doctor's visits.** Tiganda needs to practice ahead of time on dolls, so the visit will be familiar. Her first doctor was loud and fast moving. Her parents found one who moves more slowly and tells Tiganda what is going to happen next.

✤ **Eating.** Tiganda doesn't waste her limited adaptation energy on something as basic as eating. At ten months, she demanded the same blue cup and the same few foods. At two years, she always wanted her food fixed the same way—toast cut into triangles, potatoes mashed, not in a soup. At four, she helped Mom plan ahead what they would have for breakfast each day.

Being slow to adapt, she doesn't like her personal space being suddenly crowded. That made it hard to get used to a bib and a high chair.

As an intense baby, Tiganda was either not hungry at all, or starving. Sometimes she wasn't hungry when the clock said it was mealtime. If Mom got worried and pushed spoonfuls of food in her mouth, Tiganda vomited. She wasn't sick. She got upset because Mom was upset. Then her stomach got too tight to hold food. As she grew, she never felt hungry when she was really excited or sad or angry.

Tiganda needs time to wake up in the morning. And she's not hungry when she's still sleepy. She gets hungry about 9 a.m. Mom was relieved to find home daycare where Tiganda could eat her breakfast when she got hungry.

Cousin Twila, who is slow to adapt and intense like Tiganda, is *also* very sensitive. With these three traits together, she is a very picky eater. As a baby, Twila screamed if there were too many lumps in her mashed bananas. At two, she wouldn't eat a different brand of chicken noodle soup because the flavor was different.

✤ **Head banging.** When Tiganda was fourteen months old, she pulled the cat's tail. Mom said, "You can pat kitty or stroke kitty like this, but pulling kitty's tail is not okay." Tiganda reached over and again pulled kitty's tail. Mom repeated the instructions and added,

"I'm putting kitty outside so her tail won't get hurt." Tiganda was very frustrated. She really wanted to play with the kitty. She got so angry she hit her own head on the floor. Mom was horrified. She'd never seen such a thing.

Several weeks later, Mom took Tiganda's shirt off because it was bath time. Tiganda didn't want her shirt off. She was frustrated and angry! She put her own wrist in her mouth and bit so hard she left teeth marks. Again, Mom was scared. She called a temperament counselor, who said, "Many intense, slow-adapting children react this way when very frustrated. Fortunately, this phase will pass as Tiganda learns to talk instead." In the meantime, when Tiganda hit her head on the carpet, Mom talked to her in a soothing voice. One day she banged her head on the cement walkway. Mom carried her inside, while Tiganda kicked and screamed. Mom put her on her bed, where she couldn't hurt herself.

✤ **Hitting.** When Tiganda hit another child in preschool, the teacher separated her calmly and firmly. Sometimes she asks Tiganda to help the other child feel better. Getting a cool cloth for the bruise, or sitting nearby until the other child stops crying, gradually taught her how her actions affected others. Mom also taught Tiganda other things to do with an angry body, like stamp her feet. They practiced together by playing the "angry stomping game."

Now that Tiganda can talk easily, Dad helps her find words for her anger. He asks, "How were you feeling before you hit Mary?" Then he asks, "What happened *after* you hit her?" Since Tiganda turned four, he also asks, "What could you do differently next time?" Tiganda said she could stamp her feet, like in the "angry stomping game" or use her words to say, "I'm mad!" or, "Move away! You're too close."

While most children control the urge to bite and hit by the age of two and a half or three, Tiganda still has trouble sometimes at five. When strong feelings roar through Tiganda's awareness, she *can't* perceive other people's feelings. Because she has many strong feelings each day, she is often blind to the feelings of others. When she gets overwhelmed, she looses control and hits or bites.

Because Tiganda is intense and slow adapting, she gets upset if others suddenly crowd too close to her. When she is quietly playing at the doll house in preschool and other children crowd close, she strikes out and hits them. At age three, her teacher helped her learn to hold her arms out straight, and say, "Stop! This is my space right now."

✤ **Hurt feelings.** Like Tiganda, cousin Twila is also intense and slow to adapt. Twila is also very sensitive. One day, when she was four, a friend teased Twila. Being sensitive, Twila's feelings were hurt. Mom walked over to hug Twila. But Twila pushed her and yelled, "Go away! Leave me alone!" Twila crawled under the table, shouting, "I hate you. I hate my life!" Mom was surprised and confused! She didn't know this is a common reaction for children like Twila. Because Twila is slow to adapt, she doesn't like people crowding into her space—even people offering comfort. The more intense her feelings, the more she hates being crowded. Three minutes later, she crawled out, smiled, and said, "I want to go to the park." Mom was amazed at how quickly her feelings changed. Over time, Twila had learned that when she's really upset, she needs some time by herself. Fortunately, Mom stayed calm when Twila shouted at her. Later, in the park, they talked about what had happened with her friend, and about what she could do differently next time.

✤ **Moody.** Other parents are upset by Tiganda's moodiness. Her parents say she is in training for the theater. Moodiness isn't surprising. All her feelings are strong, whether happy or unhappy ones. She's never just pleased or disappointed. She's *extremely* delighted or devastated. In her early years, upsets turned into tantrums. As she approached first grade, tantrums were uncommon. Usually, she nagged and complained and sulked when things didn't go her way.

✤ **Perfectionism.** Tiganda always wants things "just so." Even at age three she had a picture in her mind of what she wanted to draw. If her drawing looked different from the picture in her mind, she cried and tore up her drawing. At six, she still had a picture in her head. But having had more practice, she could make the drawings look more like her mind pictures. Tiganda has a fast-adapting friend named Camber. Whenever life doesn't match the picture in Camber's head, he quickly changes his mind picture. But Tiganda can't change her mind pictures so quickly. She struggles, instead, to make life more like the pictures in her mind.

✤ **Separation.** Between eighteen and twenty-four months, Tiganda had some difficulty with separation. She missed Mom. But mainly, she didn't like the changes and extra transitions. Once she got to know the sitter or the school well, she was fine. Mom usually arranged several short visits to the new day care first. To make separation easier, they always use the same good-bye routine. On the way to day care they sing (to the tune of "Farmer in the Dell"): "To the sitter we will go, To the sitter we will go . . ." Then Mom sings, "I'll be back as soon as you know, I'll be back as soon as you know . . ."

When Tiganda was little, she always took her favorite pillow. Now she takes a favorite toy. At three, Tiganda liked to push Mom out the day care door. That helped her feel in control of the separation. When the sitter comes to their house, Mom gives careful instructions so the sitter will keep Tiganda's routines the same as usual. Not surprisingly, when Tiganda is sick, or tired, or when someone in the family is under stress, she is more upset by separation.

❖ **Sibling rivalry.** Tiganda was four when her baby brother was born. Mom was careful to spend special time with Tiganda. At first, Tiganda liked this baby. But then he started to crawl. He liked Tiganda and liked to be near her. He was always crawling into Tiganda's space. Tiganda didn't like that at all! She pushed him away. He cried. Mom got upset.

Dad saw that Tiganda needed space of her own. He got her a step-stool, so she could put some of her toys out of the baby's reach. He suggested Tiganda do her projects at the dining room table, or in the playpen where the baby couldn't reach her. Mom said, "You can play with your dolls on my bed during the day." When they moved into a bigger apartment, Tiganda had her own room. She was glad she could shut the door to keep the baby out.

❖ **Sleep.** For intense Tiganda, it is hard to fall asleep when muscles are tense. When Tiganda was a baby, Mom rocked and sang her to sleep. When she was a toddler, it became Dad's job to put her to bed. Tiganda didn't want to be left alone. She cried. Dad felt bad. He stayed and patted. Tiganda stayed awake to be sure he didn't leave. She begged for more stories. Dad's heart ached for her and he read more stories. The more she learned to talk, the better her reasons were for him to stay. Gradually, the bedtime ritual got longer and longer. The later she got to bed, the more tired she was, and the more difficulty she had getting to sleep the next night. Bedtime became a disaster.

Finally, they decided that Mom would put Tiganda to bed because she could stay firm and calm. Mom also knew that because Tiganda is slow to adapt, she would resist *any* change at first. But she also knew that Tiganda felt anxious when routines kept changing. Mom settled on a plan she could live with and told Tiganda ahead of time: a hug, one story, and a back rub for five minutes—then Mom would leave.

That night Tiganda cried and cried. The next night Tiganda said she had to go potty. Mom didn't let Tiganda get up to go to the bathroom. She quickly put her in a diaper and left the room. Each afternoon, Mom reminded Tiganda of the new routine. The next three nights Tiganda cried a long time. The next night, and thereafter, she went right to sleep without any fuss. Dad was amazed! Mom was glad she knew about temperament, and that a *very regular routine* is the friend of a slow adapting child.

❖ **Stomach aches and diarrhea.** Cousin Twila has the same temperament as Tiganda. She is also very sensitive. Every time Twila started a new day care or class, she complained of stomach aches. Mom thought Twila was pretending and making excuses to avoid school. So she called Twila's doctor. The doctor said, "No, she is not pretending. Twila's intense body reacts to the stress of being in a new situation. She may get some diarrhea as well as stomach aches. Take her for short periods, or several half days, so she can adjust more gradually." In June, Mom took Twila to visit her September classroom. Mom also arranged to visit with a girl one year older, who had just finished that class. The older girl told Twila all about the new teacher, the classroom rules, and what to expect. Mom and Twila talked during the summer about her September class. Twila built pictures in her head of what to expect. Because she had an accurate mind picture, her body felt better in September.

❖ **Stubbornness.** Tiganda always has a picture in her mind of what she expects to happen next. Because she's slow to adapt, it takes time to change the pictures. When Mom suddenly tells her to stop what she's doing, Tiganda's natural reaction is, "No!" Stopping right now doesn't fit the picture in her head. If Mom gets angry and punishes Tiganda for being disobedient, Tiganda gets more intense. Then she is less able to adapt. She seems even more stubborn. Fortunately, Mom has learned that mental pictures have to change before behavior can change. When others complain that Tiganda is strong willed and stubborn, Mom answers, "Tiganda does have a mind of her own. It will be useful to her when she grows up!"

❖ **Temper tantrums.** Because Tiganda has strong feelings and is slow to adapt, she started having temper tantrums around thirteen months of age. During her early years, tantrums were a daily event.

✤ *Two kinds of tantrums.* Grandma complained to Tiganda's parents, "You give in to Tiganda too much. You are spoiling her!" Dad answered, "Tiganda is special. She needs a special kind of care-taking." Then Dad explained about two different kinds of tantrums.

Temperament Tantrum

Purpose: To release emotional tension. Is an expression of child's temperament.

Cause: Needs food, sleep, or exercise.

Has run out of adaptation energy.

Is overwhelmed by too many things going on (sensitive child).

Parent action: Plan ahead to avoid such tantrums in the future. You are respecting temperament, not "giving in."

Manipulative Tantrum

Purpose: To control other people.

Cause: Wants to play *right now* with the toy someone else has.

Wants crayons to color on the wall.

Parent action: Calmly and firmly hold the line. Let these tantrums run their course.

Tiganda's parents started to pay close attention to her intensity level. Here's what they learned:

Level 1. *Intensity beginning to rise.* Tiganda frowns, stops making eye contact, gets a special "look" in her eyes, voice gets louder or higher, talks faster, or is unable to talk.

Level 2. *Intensity rising fast.* Tiganda yells, says bad or hurtful words, make threats.

Level 3. *Meltdown.* Tiganda is screaming, throwing things, hitting, biting, kicking.

Sometimes Tiganda flashes instantly to Level 3. Usually it's late in the day, she's been short of sleep, or the day has used up more than the usual amount of adaptation energy. If Tiganda starts kicking Mom or throwing things in the living room, Mom carries her to her room or out to the patio. Those may be safer places for a tantrum. Mom doesn't require Tiganda to stay for a certain length of time. Instead, she calmly states the goal: "You can come back when you are in control." If Tiganda storms out too soon, Mom calmly repeats the goal:

"Tiganda, you are not in control yet. Let's try again." Mom guides her back.

Repeatedly carrying an intense, slow to adapt child back to her room often escalates the anger. Families with children like Tiganda try different ways to contain damaging anger. Some stand and hold the door shut, but this can become a power struggle. Others lock the door. Most find the best solution is prevention. Sometimes, during tantrums, Tiganda broke a toy. Mom put it in the "toy hospital" for a day until they repaired it together.

Tantrums really upset Tiganda's parents. Mom used to say to herself, "Tiganda is so difficult!" or, "Why can't I be more patient?" She felt anger, blame, or guilt. So whenever Tiganda had strong feelings and a tantrum, Mom had strong feelings, too. In order to stay off the intensity spiral, Mom needed ways to stay calm. First, she timed how long Tiganda's tantrums lasted. Then when a new tantrum started, she could say to herself, "There goes the tiger's roar. The noise will last for about twenty minutes." Because Mom knew what to expect, she felt more in control. She also started saying different things to herself during Tiganda's tantrums, such as, "Life is tough when you are little," or, "For someone with strong feelings, like Tiganda, life is very hard." Avoiding blame, anger, and guilt helped Mom stay calmer during tantrums.

When Tiganda screams in a store, Mom waits. Or she carries Tiganda away from the crowd or to the car. When strangers give angry looks, Mom says to herself, "If you had raised a child like Tiganda, you would understand!" When Dad couldn't carry Tiganda because of a broken arm, he carried a folded sign in his pocket that read, "Temper Tantrum in Progress."

✤ **Toilet training.** Because Tiganda works from pictures in her head, Mom found opportunities for her to watch others in the bathroom. Mom also read books about using the potty. It was a good start. But unfortunately, Mom learned the hard way that Tiganda would go at her very own speed. When Tiganda was three and a half most of her friends were already trained. Tiganda showed no interest. Being slow to adapt, it's hard to make transitions from playing to getting to the potty whenever her unpredictable body makes demands. When wearing diapers, Tiganda's mind is in control of her activities. Letting her body be in control is hard.

But Mom was anxious for progress. So she decided to move ahead with toilet training. She told Tiganda to sit on the potty after breakfast and before her bath. When she saw Tiganda squat and push, she said, "Let's go do that in the toilet." With Mom's request for immediate action, Tiganda's intensity went up. As her intensity rose, so did the tension in her body. So when they arrived at the potty, she was too tense to let go. Mom tried this approach for several days. And Tiganda went several days with no bowel movement. When she did have one, it was large and very painful. After that, Tiganda was afraid to go. Now Mom and daughter were caught in a vicious cycle of pain and holding back. The struggle went on for weeks. Mom finally decided to get help from Tiganda's doctor.

Mom didn't know children of this temperament type often aren't ready for toilet training until they are between three and a half and four and a half years old. By that age, life has become more routine. There are fewer surprises than at age two or three. Mom wished she had known not to push Tiganda to be like her friends.

Twila's mom took a different approach because she knew that Twila needed to be in control. Mom read books and arranged times to watch others in the bathroom. But she didn't pressure Twila. Sometimes she said, "It will be nice when you can use the potty. Remember the story we read?" Her hardest job was finding child care which accepted individual differences. A program that was terrific in many ways would not accept children in diapers. Mom said to herself, "In this town, it's not easy having a child who runs on her own track." When Twila turned four, she began to seem interested. So several times a week, Mom asked in the morning, "Do you want to wear diapers or big girl pants today?" Gradually, Twila chose big girl pants more and more often.

Not surprisingly, children like Tiganda don't toilet train when life is in uproar. It is also common to backslide when family changes and stresses are using up adaptation energy.

❖ **Vomiting**. One day at eighteen months, Tiganda was tired and frustrated. She had three tantrums in a row. Mom decided to put Tiganda in her crib and leave her until she fell asleep. Tiganda screamed until her body was very tight like a stretched rubberband. Her stomach got so tight she vomited. A month later, Tiganda vomited when she didn't want to be in her car seat. Then she vomited when Mom hurried to put her in the stroller. Mom felt really embarrassed when Tiganda vomited in the shopping mall. Gradually, Tiganda learned that she could *make* her stomach so tight that she vomited. One day, Dad really needed to leave a party early. Tiganda didn't want to go and started to scream. Then Tiganda tightened her stomach and vomited! Dad had to stay longer to clean up. Dad called the temperament counselor, who said, "Vomiting usually happens when families get caught in intensity spirals." As Tiganda's parents learned to work with their own intensity, and with Tiganda's, the vomiting stopped.

✤ **Weaning.** Not surprisingly, Tiganda weaned later than other children. She needed lots of time to see others use cups and to drink from one herself, before she was ready to set aside breast and bottle.

Mom first introduced a bottle and cup right after lunch. Tiganda wasn't really hungry then and was more adaptable at that time of day. Tiganda most needed breast or bottle while slowly waking up in the morning and to calm her tense body at bedtime. *Mom* didn't want to give up the evening bottle when Tiganda was a year old. It made bedtime *much* easier. However, the dentist said that sucking on a bottle in bed could cause tooth decay. So Mom took the bottle away as soon as Tiganda fell asleep. Unfortunately, Tiganda woke later and fussed for her bottle. So Mom gradually added more water and less milk to Tiganda's bottle. In a few weeks, it was plain water. Then she didn't have to worry about Tiganda's teeth.

Mom's friends said Tiganda should give up the bottle by age two. But Mom said, "Two will be one of the hardest years of her life. She'll need all the help she can get." When Tiganda turned four, Dad felt embarrassed that Tiganda still had a bottle, so he made a new rule: "Bottles stay in the bedroom." And, he said to himself, "I'm sure she won't take it to high school."

Words to Help Your Child Live with High Intensity

Parent	Child
If you lovingly tell your child:	Your child learns to say:
You have big, strong feelings.	*I have big strong feelings.*
Your feelings are strong and fast like racing horses.	*My feelings are strong and fast like racing horses.*
How fast are your horses running right now?	*How fast are my horses running right now?*
What can calm your horses now?	*What can calm my horses now?*
You're learning to control your racing horses.	*I'm learning to control my racing horses.*
You can think and plan better when your horses are resting.	*I can think and plan better when my horses are resting.*

🖼 Words to Help Your Child Live with Low Adaptability

Parent	Child
If you lovingly tell your child:	Your child learns to say:
You need time to change the picture in your head.	*I need time to change the picture in my head.*
You like little things to stay the same so you have energy to make important changes.	*I like little things to stay the same so I have energy to make important changes.*
You like to do things at the same time and in the same way because then you feel more peaceful.	*I like to do things at the same time and in the same way because then I feel more peaceful.*
In a few days (weeks), you'll be comfortable with this new situation.	*In a few days (weeks), I'll be comfortable with this new situation.*

Tiganda Tiger shares these behaviors with other children profiled in this book. For more help, see the pages noted here:

Testing limits, pp. 59-60   Sleep, bedtime, pp. 57-58, 98
Sibling rivalry, pp. 97-98

Teach Your Child How to Control Intense Feelings

With help along the way from their parents and teachers, intense children can begin to understand their own intensity by the age of four or five.

From the beginning, you need to accept their need to let off steam by stomping feet, punching pillows, jumping up and down, and so on. These actions are not (necessarily) signs of defiance. Refer to the temperament or manipulative tantrums charts if in doubt (page 77).

Use words to describe and measure feelings. Help children learn to *notice and measure* the intensity of their feelings. As they approach age three, tell them what you see: "I see your feelings are getting big because you are talking louder." Talk about big feelings *after the fact:* "Your feelings were really strong when you threw the truck! [Or splashed all the water out of the tub, or happily hugged a cousin so hard she cried.] Let's practice something else you could do the next time your feelings are so big."

Use images to describe feelings. Around age four, look for an image your child likes. Are feelings like a can of soda (pop) that is quiet, or fizzy and spraying all over? Do an experiment (in a safe manner) to show your child what you mean. He'll love to watch that demonstration! How about a pot of water that is cool, warm, or boiling? Maybe flames in the fireplace, a race car, a motorcycle, or running horses evoke the image. One five-year-old described her feelings as a volcano. Help children notice when feelings are starting to get bigger or faster. "Are you feeling wound up? Revved up? How fast are your horses racing? Are you about to explode?" Praise children for noticing and describing their own intensity.

Around age five or six, get more specific: "On a scale of one to ten, how fizzy are your feelings right now?" Explain that one is calm and ten is out of control.

Identify ways to calm strong feelings. Feelings get out of control when they get big, or reach levels nine or ten. Plan ahead with four- and five-year-olds. What will calm down middle-sized feelings so they don't grow too big? A break? A mini-recess? A hug? A bath? A walk? Playing quietly with a favorite toy?

When the time comes, ask, "What did we think would help when the horses start racing?" Support and praise the child's efforts to keep feelings in control.

BeiLing Bluebird

The Active, Easily Frustrated Child

BeiLing Bluebird is always on the move and in a hurry to get somewhere. He goes places and does things. He spreads his wings and flies toward independence. On the other hand, he gets discouraged easily. He depends on adults for help. A bird that flies quickly and lightly, he flits between independence and dependence: two flaps forward and one flap back.

Child shows: Activity, high and Frustration reaction, easily discouraged and frustrated

Keys to Living with the Active, Easily Frustrated Child

BeiLing's energy pushes him up and out. Then frustration pulls him down and back. Independence, then dependence; a continual dance of two steps forward, one step back. Don't compare his milestones (weaning, toilet training, etc.) with other children's. BeiLing is on his own schedule.

Children like BeiLing need positive ways to handle frustration. His parents show him, repeatedly, how to take a more positive view of problem solving. They patiently teach him skills to deal with frustration that will last a lifetime.

❖ **Break tasks into small, easy parts.** Tell him, "To put the puzzle together, first find all the corner pieces." When he reaches age three or four, ask him, "How can we break this job into little parts?" Teach him how to think that way.

❖ **Offer frequent encouragement.** *Praise effort, not just results:* "I see you're really working hard at that," or, "Good! You're going to go back to try again." Praise partial success: "Look! We've put all the big books on the shelf."

❖ **Plan ways to work around frustration.** BeiLing stops when he is too frustrated. You will have to serve up frustration in small, manageable pieces. Plan out the *number of frustrating things you fit into each day.* Allow him some choice in how much frustration he takes on: "Do you want me to put the straw in the juice box, or do you want to?" Do frustrating tasks when he is at his best, probably in the morning. Be sure he gets a good night's sleep.

❖ **Share tasks.** BeiLing is a team player. Work with this natural tendency. When he reaches age three or four, make agreements with him about what he will do and what you will do: "We need to pick up all the blocks. Do you want to pick up red ones or blue ones? I'll pick up the others."

❖ **Teach him how to ask for specific help.** "You are hurting the baby. When you are bored or need help or attention, tell me with words." Encourage him to say what he *can* do and then ask for the exact help he needs: "I can put this circle in the puzzle, but not this square." He will feel more capable and other people will be more willing to help him.

Parent Care

❖ **Avoid burnout.** Because of BeiLing's energy, his parents get worn out. When he was little, his parents took turns so each could sleep.

Later, they set up a baby-sitting exchange with other families. Sometimes BeiLing's mom feels she is the master of ceremonies at a three-ring circus. As the folk saying goes, all children would benefit from being raised in a village—especially BeiLing!

❖ **Be consistent.** When you decide on a plan (like time-out after poking the baby), give *yourself* a gold star for following through.

❖ **Expect these children to complain!** BeiLing Bluebird is often discouraged. Life feels harder for him than it does for other children. He whines more than others even if he has the best of parents. Whining is a way to get adults involved when life feels too frustrating. For parent relief, plan activities ahead, like play groups and daycare. Provide easy home activities—such as large cardboard building blocks, big pillows to climb on, and water play areas. Avoid frustrating video games or crafts that require skilled finger work. Demonstrate strong and whiny voices. Encourage him to use a strong voice.

❖ **Keep afternoons and evenings easy and predictable.** As the day goes by, children like BeiLing Bluebird get emotionally worn out from the day's frustrations. They are less able to entertain themselves. They may act out more on returning home than they did during school. Easy afternoon rituals can help.

But BeiLing still has energy to burn off, even though he can't handle more frustration. So Dad parks two blocks from nursery school so that BeiLing can run to the car, where a snack is waiting. On arriving home, Mom and BeiLing do an exercise video together. Three days a week, Dad pays a junior high school student to play with BeiLing while he fixes dinner. The other two days, BeiLing dances to his favorite music or rocks on his rocking horse in the corner of the kitchen.

🔲 Learning Style

Active toddlers have more energy than skill. So they run and jump and climb. As they get older, they gladly put their energy into active games.

BeiLing Bluebird learns by *doing*, not by watching. He learns to get dressed by dressing; to pour milk by pouring. He learns colors as he scribbles with crayons. He'll most easily learn letters by tracing his finger over their shapes. He'll most easily learn math by playing with counting blocks or interactive computer games. Teachers call his learning "kinesthetic." BeiLing needs ways to make the physical prac-tice easier. First, he learned to put big Duplo® blocks together, then smaller Lego® blocks. He learned to fasten big buttons before trying small ones.

Everyone learns better when calm, not anxious. Frustration makes BeiLing feel anxious. Feeling *afraid of becoming frustrated* also makes him anxious. So he learns best when there is a trusted parent, teacher, or fellow student nearby, to help when he needs it. BeiLing is a team learner. Like everyone else, BeiLing learns better when his mind is fresh. That's usually in the morning.

✤ **Child care/Preschool.** Because of his high energy, BeiLing learned to crawl, walk, and jump sooner than others his age. As a result, he likes playing with older children who match his energy and physical skill. BeiLing also behaves better with older children. If he doesn't fol-low their rules, they won't let him play. So Mom looked for a school with active, older children and with an energetic teacher who could match BeiLing's pace. This school also had easy, *planned* activities to help use up energy. Mornings started with a walk in the neighborhood or dancing if the weather was too bad. In the afternoon, they had "track time," when the active children circled the yard on their big wheels. There was plenty of outdoor space, a sandbox, and water play in the summer. How did Mom know when she had found the right school? She could see that another child with similar tempera-ment was happy and well managed by the teachers.

✤ *Adjusting.* Adjusting to a new school was not easy for BeiLing. The first part was getting used to a new place. Daddy took him to visit ahead of time. At first, he stayed so BeiLing could get used to where things were, and how things there worked. That was the easy part. The harder part was getting along without Mommy or Daddy.

BeiLing missed Mommy and Daddy at school. He worked extra hard to take care of himself at school. By the time he got home, he'd had as much frustration as he could handle in one day. Having been away, he also wondered if Mommy and Daddy still loved him. So he needed much more help that usual. He wanted Daddy to feed him dinner and Mommy to put his pajamas on. After a few weeks, BeiLing learned that his teacher was a good helper, too. He began to like school and didn't miss Mommy and Daddy so much. Gradually, he was again able to do more for himself at home.

✤ *Class clown.* Like BeiLing, his sister BeiShi is active and easily frus-trated. BeiShi is also extremely curious. When she gets discouraged *or* bored in class, she makes the other children laugh with her jokes and funny faces. That's easier and more fun than hard or boring tasks at her desk. Without realizing it, the teacher began to stand nearby to keep BeiShi out of trouble. Fortunately for BeiShi, the teacher is now close when BeiShi needs help. In first grade, the teacher put BeiShi's desk next to his own. The teacher asked a patient, helpful student to sit on the other side of BeiShi. The more comfortable BeiShi felt, the less she clowned around.

 Common Behavior Issues

✤ **Anger.** The Bluebird children are often upset with their mom. BeiLing hates waiting for the help and support he needs. BeiShi (who is much like BeiLing *and also very curious*) is frustrated by the limits Mom sets. Mom knows their moods are better when they have enough sleep and have the frequent snacks they need. She also knows they need more help after a day's worth of frustrations. Especially at the end of the day, Mom tries to provide enjoyable activities that are more fun than frustrating.

✤ **Blaming others.** All small children blame their parents when things go wrong. BeiLing blames more than usual. He gives up easily and stops trying; when he doesn't get what he wants, he feels helpless. He doesn't feel in control of his surroundings. He believes other people have more control. So when something goes wrong, it must be *their* fault—his friend, or teacher, or Mom. The more he learns to work with his own temperament, the less he needs to blame others. (But don't expect him to stop entirely, or soon.)

✤ **Boredom.** BeiLing can't stick with things as well as other children can. When his energy makes him move, he goes on to something else. When something gets hard he goes on to something else. He can't handle painting or complicated Lego® projects. He quickly tries lots of different things and then feels bored. His solution is to climb on the table, pull over the plants, get into cupboards and drawers. That makes life more exciting! He feels powerful when he has an effect on the world. The result is that children like BeiLing simply need more time, attention, and help than other children.

✤ **Channel surfing through life.** BeiLing's sister, BeiShi, is active, easily discouraged, *and* curious. She's *always* on the move to find interesting, easy things to do. If it's *either* boring or frustrating, she moves on to something else. In her own way, she's doing what everyone does—looking for things she feels good about doing. If she's tired, ill, or under stress, she gets even more discouraged. Then she moves even faster from one thing to another.

❖ **Danger.** BeiLing's energy takes him everywhere, fast. That's why he crashes into safety limits more often than slow-moving children. He isn't really *trying* to drive his parents crazy. He crawled along the top edge of the sofa and tried climbing up the living room bookcases. He climbed the stepladder Dad left out after changing a light bulb. He ran and slipped into the goldfish pond in the park. He climbed inside the ice cream display in the grocery store. (Dad rounded the corner and found him peering out at him through the glass door.)

No wonder Mom and Dad worried about safety! They decided they needed a safety plan. First, they made a list with three parts:

1. *Life-threatening or serious injury*
Running in the street or parking lot
Falling into Rapid River
Falling on top of the floor furnace

2. *Injury, pain, possible broken bones, but not life-threatening*
Falling off the kitchen counter
Falling off the stepladder
Touching the oven door with fingertips

3. *Nuisance for Mom and Dad*
Falling in the fishpond
Pouring out the cat litter
Making messes with food and drink

They covered the floor furnace with a solid wooden frame and decided not to visit Rapid River again soon. That left just one big rule: "Always hold on to my hand in the street. In the grocery parking lot, hold hands, or hold the grocery cart, or the car." Mom felt much calmer and more relaxed when she knew only a very few things were really, really dangerous.

Mom and Dad know BeiLing will test the rules many times. Suddenly yelling, "Stop!" doesn't work very well. But sometimes they do use that strong, stern voice if BeiLing runs too close to the street without holding their hands. They try to use a calmer voice at other times, so BeiLing will learn that streets are more dangerous than pouring out the kitty litter. Usually, Dad simply takes BeiLing's hand and says, "We hold hands in the street."

Gradually Mom and Dad learned to remind BeiLing of safety rules ahead of time: "What will you do to stay safe when we get out of the car? Sometimes they calmly practiced safety rules before reading bedtime stories: "What do you need to do to be safe in the parking lot?" This helped BeiLing get the rule more clearly in his mind. They also learned to tell BeiLing about new safety rules ahead of time. "We're going to cross the bridge. The rail is for looking through, not for climbing on." Of course, they expected him to test the new rule, so they stayed close to him. When he started to climb the railing, they took him down and repeated the rule.

Some days BeiLing was drawn like a magnet to danger. Dad called this the "danger flag." It meant BeiLing needed more ways to run off his energy. Mom didn't want BeiLing away more hours in day care. But it became clear that BeiLing needed to burn off more energy. They bought more tapes for dancing. They got cold weather clothes for going out in winter. They also found malls, airports, and other places to exercise in winter. They arranged more play time with other children.

✦ **Delayed speech**. Because of his energy, BeiLing uses big muscles. Talking uses small muscles in the mouth. When BeiLing was little, he pointed or led Dad to what he wanted. Mom and Dad helped BeiLing use different signals for things he wanted—like sucking with his lips when he wanted a bottle. They also practiced naming things when BeiLing was relaxed, while riding in the car or looking at bedtime books. Gradually, BeiLing used more words during the day.

✦ **Dependence and demands for help**. BeiLing needs help with more things, for longer periods of time than other children do. BeiLing comes to a standstill with problems that other children hardly notice, like pulling sleeves right side out before putting on a sweater. This is especially true when he's tired after a whole day of dealing with other frustrations. Sometimes food and rest can restore his active, independent side. Mom has learned to plan difficult activities, like a doctor's appointment, in the mornings. BeiLing is at his best then. Mom plans easy activities in the afternoon, like dancing to videos.

As Dad learned more about temperament, he found that working as "a team" was better than nagging. BeiLing feels much more secure when someone else is around to lend a hand in case the going gets tough. Instead of trying to push BeiLing away before he was ready, Mom and Dad decided to stick by him until *he* was ready to be on his own. So, for example, when dressing, BeiLing did one side while Mom did the other. From time to time, Mom said, "You'll know when you are ready to do this by yourself." One day, many months later, BeiLing *was* ready to get dressed by himself. Dad and BeiLing set the table together. Dad tells him, "You're a team player. You like working with other people."

BeiLing's friend has a temperament much like BeiLing's, except Brandon's body rhythms are also very irregular. He gets tired and hungry at different times of day. When he is awake and well fed, he is very independent. When he is either tired or hungry, his dependent, clingy side shows more than usual. His mom has more difficulty than BeiLing's in predicting how any particular day will go.

✤ **Eating.** A bluebird is always on the move. BeiLing burns energy quickly and gets hungry often. Mom keeps easy, healthy snacks on a shelf where BeiLing can stand and eat them—crackers, cubes of cheese, orange sections, or defrosted frozen peas. BeiLing can fly in and snack like a jet plane that refuels in mid-flight. However, for safety, Mom taught him to stop and eat, rather than run with food in his mouth. Mom didn't want crumbs all over the house, either. So whenever BeiLing left the kitchen with food, Mom brought him back to the kitchen, saying, "Food stays in the kitchen." BeiLing screamed. Finally, he learned that he could only eat in the kitchen. Usually he eats half his dinner while dancing around the kitchen as Mom cooks. He's able to sit for only a few minutes at the family dinner table. As he grew, he became able to sit for longer periods.

When BeiLing is tired or really hungry, new foods are just one more frustration. Mom has learned to offer new foods when BeiLing is rested and only a little hungry. Sometimes, when he's really tired, he doesn't eat any dinner at all. BeiLing got so frustrated and anxious wanting the dessert that he couldn't eat his dinner. So Mom decided to serve a tiny, nutritious dessert at the *beginning* of dinner as part of the routine.

This on-the-go and backwards meal plan has been hard for Dad. He wasn't raised this way. But Mom is very active and remembers how she hated sitting at the table every night when she was little. A meal plan that suits BeiLing's temperament means less stress for everyone. After BeiLing had settled into kindergarten, they started having one special family dinner each week. They lit candles and everyone sat at the table together. By then, BeiLing had so much to say about school that he was content to sit at the table for ten or fifteen minutes.

✤ **Friendly with strangers.** Because BeiLing is active and likes to talk, he meets people easily. He's also learned that many different adults can help when he gets stuck—Mommy and Daddy, Auntie and Uncle, Grandma and Grandpa, baby sitters, and teachers. One day, Mom was late picking BeiLing up after school. BeiLing was by himself, talking with a total stranger. At first, Mom was frightened. She hadn't thought that BeiLing might rely on *any* adult for help. Mom needed to talk with BeiLing about safety and strangers. People to ask for help were teachers, policemen, or store clerks. He should never get in a stranger's car, because Mom would not know where he was, and Mom would worry. Though Mom had been frightened that day, she knew BeiLing's trait would be helpful in adulthood. "BeiLing automatically connects with other people to get things done. He will be a terrific networker!" she told herself reassuringly.

✧ **Friends, trouble with.** Because BeiLing is so active, he can run, skip, and hop much better than other children his age. Therefore, he prefers to be around older children to practice and learn more physical skills. If he lived in a small village, he would naturally play with active, older children.

But getting along with friends is not always easy. Early on, he had more trouble sharing toys. Waiting for his turn was hard! He got frustrated when the rules of a game got in his way. Other children sometimes called him a "baby" or a "cheater." They didn't want him on their team. Gradually, he found out that if he wanted to play with the older children he had to follow the rules. Playing with older children was a good way to learn.

When BeiLing turned four, Dad talked about being part of a team. "On a team you'll need to wait your turn." They talked about how hard it is to wait. They thought of things to do while waiting. For example, in kick ball, he could practice kicking imaginary balls while he waited his turn. Dad and BeiLing keep talking about how team players act. Dad encourages him and knows that with time he'll be able to be a better sport.

✧ **Help, begging for help then refusing.** There is a constant battle going on inside BeiLing: the active, independent side fights with his easily discouraged side. He cries, "Mommy, Mommy, I can't reach the toothpaste!" Then when Mommy reaches for the toothpaste, BeiLing screams, "No! I want to do it myself!" It's always tempting to step in and do things for BeiLing. But life goes more smoothly when Mom asks outloud, "I wonder what would work . . . " It's often helpful *to remind BeiLing of what has worked before:* "When you pull the stool to the sink, you still can't reach. Yesterday you pushed the chair over. That worked better."

✤ **Lying.** "Have you brushed your teeth, BeiLing? Have you cleaned your room? Have you done your homework?" BeiLing knew the answer Mom and Dad wanted to hear. He didn't want to upset them. So he said, "Yes!" Then Mom got angry because BeiLing's answers weren't true. Dad said, "In this country, we have a Fifth Amendment. Adults don't have to say bad things about themselves. So why do we expect BeiLing to?" So instead, Dad started saying, "BeiLing, let's go brush our teeth," or, "Your room needs cleaning. Let's go do it," or, "Come do your homework near me, so you can tell me if you need help." BeiLing felt much better.

✤ **Moodiness.** BeiLing is moody because his life is difficult. Some children naturally glide through frustrations. But for BeiLing, frustrations are big, ugly bumps in his path. Not surprisingly, he is especially moody when he hasn't had enough rest.

✤ **Pleasure seeking.** BeiLing is naturally drawn to things that are fun. He sticks with things as long as they bring more fun than frustration. He's much less interested in finishing a project than in having fun along the way. In our busy, workaholic world, we need people to remind us to live in the present and have fun along the way.

Suitable Toys and Activities for
Young, Active, Easily Frustrated Children

Dancing and jumping to music; walks around the neighborhood or park; sand box, big wheel, large kick balls, simple puzzles, finger paints, rocking horse, bouncer ball, wagon, water table and toys, crayons and large pieces of paper, large cardboard boxes, cars and trucks, dolls, stuffed animals, crib mattress for jumping on, play dough

Activities for Older Children

Jazz, modern dance, tether ball, swimming, martial arts, hiking, bicycling

Toys and Activities that May Be Too Frustrating

Complicated puzzles, detailed crafts, small Legos® and other construction toys with lots of small pieces, small blocks, long stories/books, cooking (measuring, mixing, pouring, cutting), activity and coloring books, ballet, baseball

✦ **Running off.** BeiLing's sister BeiShi is active; she's also *very* curious. BeiLing is often content to go to the same places and do the same things. But BeiShi is drawn like a magnet to everything new and different. She's a world-class explorer. Mom needs a full-time nanny on roller skates! Whenever they go out, BeiShi automatically bolts off to check out interesting sights. Mom has learned to limit trips to frustrating places like stores. Early on, she used a harness when they went for a walk. (Active BeiShi hated sitting in a stroller.) As BeiShi got older, Mom used the harness only as a consequence of running too far ahead or into the street.

At home, they played a game. They took turns telling each other, "Stop!" and "Go!" This was fun and practice for going on adventures. When BeiShi turned four, the practice paid off. Mom could really use the game when she needed it outdoors.

✦ **Self-esteem, low.** When something becomes frustrating, BeiLing leaves it and moves on to something else. That way he spends less time feeling frustrated and discouraged. Moving on gets him out of painful feelings.

Gradually, around age four, BeiLing began to notice that his friends could do many things he couldn't. They could pour juice, ride big wheels on smaller paths, and do puzzles. He began to think there was something wrong with him. He gradually decided that he must not be as smart as the other children. He felt bad about himself.

Fortunately, BeiLing's parents realized early on that BeiLing was having trouble with self-esteem. They knew BeiLing was just as smart as the other children, but BeiLing didn't *practice* as much as they did. Practicing came naturally to other children, but not to BeiLing. And because he didn't practice as much, he couldn't do as much. Here are things they did to help:

Describe BeiLing's experience. Mom stopped saying, "Oh, that's easy. Just do it!" Instead, she *reported what she saw*: "That looks hard. That looks *really* hard!" or, "That looks easy for you to do!" She also taught the words "discouraged" and "frustrated," so that BeiLing could identify those feelings. When BeiLing looked especially discouraged or frustrated, Dad said, "It's okay to be discouraged. Lots of people get discouraged. What counts is what you do next." Gradually, BeiLing found he had new ways to talk about his life. Then his family could talk about things BeiLing needed help with and things he could do alone.

The "Can Do" chart. When BeiLing turned four, Mom got an idea. She made a chart and taped it to the wall where BeiLing could see it.

The "Can Do" Chart		
Easy	**Hard**	**Too hard**
Can do alone	Do together	Get help
Take off toothpaste cap	*Set table*	*Put cap on toothpaste*
Put on socks	*Feed the cat*	*Use can opener*

Whenever Mom and BeiLing read the chart, they always started with things BeiLing could do, which helped build his confidence.

BeiLing told Mom things to write (or draw, or paste a picture of) in each column. They kept looking for ways to divide things into small, easy parts. One day Dad held the can opener. BeiLing squeezed it tight while Dad opened the can. They moved the can opener to the "do together" column.

At their weekly family meeting, they talked about the chart. BeiLing told Mom when to move something to a new column. BeiLing felt proud when he moved things to the "easy" column. When he was four and a half, BeiLing wanted to turn the "Can Do" chart into a star chart. Each week he picked something from the "easy" column. Every time he did it by himself that week, Dad gave him a star.

Learn to practice. Dad helped BeiLing practice a little bit at a time. He'd say, "Let's set the timer for three minutes and practice using scissors."

As BeiLing learned to practice, he learned to do more and more. Slowly, he started feeling better about himself. He learned he was as smart as the other children. Gradually, BeiLing learned he didn't have to *avoid* challenges. He just needed to take them in small, steady steps.

BeiLing's neighbor Brandon has a temperament much like BeiLing's. He too began to think he wasn't very smart. Brandon became more and more discouraged. In first grade, other children were printing their names. For Brandon, it was still hard to make letters. So he decided, "Why even try? I'm not smart like they are." His papers were often blank or messy. He felt embarrassed turning them in. His teacher frowned when she picked up his papers. Because Brandon felt embarrassed, he would say things that weren't true, like,

"Jennifer was talking so I couldn't do my work." Brandon wasn't so fortunate as BeiLing, whose parents helped him understand how to work with temperament.

❖ **Self-soothing.** How does a flitting bird relax? BeiLing sucks his thumb, rubs his belly button, and twists his hair. These are active *and* relaxing. One day, Auntie found BeiLing masturbating in the middle of the living room floor. She said, "BeiLing, the place to do that is in private, in your own room. That's where big people do it." Mom helped BeiLing find soothing things he could do in public, without getting teased. Rocking horses and swings are great, but aren't always available. BeiLing could sit and rest his elbow on the table with his index finger against his lips. Then he could run his tongue back and forth along his finger. He could also hold his wrist and stroke the under side of it with his thumb.

No one thinks well when he's anxious. Frustration makes BeiLing anxious. When BeiLing turned five, Mom asked, "How do you feel inside when things aren't working out?" BeiLing answered, "All tight and wiggly." Mom then suggested, "When you feel tight and wiggly inside, you could take a break or get some help." BeiLing decided that when he needed a break, he would skip around the room three times. (Tarita Turtle, who is less active but also easily frustrated, pets the cat or sings a song when she needs a break.)

❖ **Separation.** There are two issues related to separation.

❖ *Clinging to Mom.* Even as an infant, BeiLing got frustrated. He didn't just wait for milk, he cried until it came. He got really annoyed when he couldn't quite sit up yet, couldn't quite crawl, or couldn't quite reach the toy he wanted. His life felt out of control; he felt helpless. At such times, he needed someone to take those bad feelings away. Better yet, he needed someone to *keep* those feelings away. Fortunately for BeiLing, Mom learned how to predict and prevent frustration. If he wasn't going to nurse, she warmed BeiLing a bottle just before he woke up from his nap. She propped him up when he wanted to sit. She saw the look in BeiLing's eye and passed the desired toy. Mom could read BeiLing's smallest cues. BeiLing loved it! He wanted Mom close by, always. Not surprisingly, if Mom wasn't around, BeiLing's cry told the whole world he was upset. Between seven and nine months of age, BeiLing began to cry every time Mom disappeared into another room. At that age, BeiLing had no way to know whether Mom would ever come back. Mom began to sing or talk loudly whenever she went into another room. Then BeiLing knew she was close by.

Fortunately, BeiLing had gotten used to one regular sitter well before he turned nine months. Mom had started leaving him for very short periods. Like Mom, this sitter learned to read BeiLing's cues. BeiLing felt comfortable with either Mom or his sitter.

Dad worked long hours. Because he spent less time with BeiLing, he couldn't read him as well as Mom. Mom told him BeiLing's private little signals. For example, he lifted his chin when he wanted to be picked up. But there were so many little signals that Dad couldn't read them all. Whenever BeiLing was with him, he cried and called for Mom. Dad felt hurt. BeiLing didn't appreciate how hard Dad tried. Around age three, things got much better. Now BeiLing could use words to tell Dad what he wanted.

✦ *Baby sitters and day care.* As a toddler and preschooler, BeiLing found it easier to go to the sitter's house than to stay home with a sitter. Because he's active, he likes new adventures in interesting places. Mom made sure BeiLing had a reminder of home. As a baby, BeiLing had his favorite blanket. At age three, Mom posted a family picture in the back of BeiLing's cubby at preschool. Sometimes BeiLing took a special toy as well. At age five, BeiLing's lunch box is usually a good enough reminder of home.

Starting with another new sitter or day care is hard for BeiLing. Would the new caretaker be as helpful as Mommy? At first, he cried every time he got frustrated, and Mom wasn't there to help him. Mommy told Noreen, the teacher, about the things that were hard, like getting a sweater on. Noreen said, "Whenever you need help, BeiLing, I'll help you."

Gradually, BeiLing learned that Noreen was a good helper. As he trusted Noreen more, he missed Mom less. But special days like field trips could bring unexpected frustrations. It helped to talk ahead of time with Mom and the teacher, so that as much as possible, he knew what to expect.

Even though BeiLing cries or complains at the time, Mom always tells him ahead of time that she is leaving. She doesn't want BeiLing to *always* be worried about when she might leave. Not surprisingly, BeiLing misses Mom even more during the evening, when he's already had a day full of frustrations.

Still at age five, BeiLing hated to see Mom on the phone. Mom didn't like interruptions, and BeiLing never knew how long the call would last. How would BeiLing get help? So they worked out a plan. After that, Mom asked, "Do you need any help before I call my friend?" or, "What's something easy and fun you can do near me while I'm on the phone?" They also set up hand signals, so when the phone rang, Mom could signal BeiLing if the call would be short, long, or unknown. Everyone felt better.

❖ **Sibling rivalry.** When baby BeiBei arrived, BeiLing's temperament didn't change. He was still easily frustrated. His shirt was too tight to fit over his head. He couldn't find his favorite teddy. But Mom and Dad were so busy since BeiBei came. He hated hearing, "Just a minute, BeiLing." How could he get their attention right away? Gradually, BeiLing discovered a quick way to get Mom's attention. If he bumped BeiBei, or squeezed his hand hard, Mom came in a hurry! Mom would be angry, but at least she'd come. Mom said, "When you need help, come take my hand, or tell me you need help. Don't hurt BeiBei when you need help. When you hurt the baby, I don't feel like helping you." Mom said this many times. BeiLing tried it out and found it *did* work better to take Mom's hand and ask for help.

Mom wanted to give BeiLing extra hugs to show him love. But busy BeiLing never had time for hugs before bedtime. Relaxing wasn't his way of getting close. So Mom looked for easy ways that BeiLing could help her. BeiLing could go get diapers and bottles. He helped Mom sort laundry and stuff clothes into the clothes dryer. He helped Dad put plastic dishes in the dish washer. He made funny faces to keep BeiBei happy and he fetched his ball. Mom always *asked*, "BeiLing, can you help me . . . ?" Sometimes BeiLing didn't help. But when he did, Mom said, "Thank you. You're such a good helper! Now we can have more time together." (Even though BeiLing's jobs didn't always save time for Mom, they helped BeiLing feel important and stay out of trouble.)

Mom didn't get angry at baby BeiBei as often as she got angry at BeiLing. As the years went by, his parents complimented BeiBei for getting dressed all by himself, talking in a grown-up voice instead of whining, sitting quietly at the table, finishing his chores without being reminded. It was easy for him to get praise and happy attention from Mom and Dad. BeiBei got more compliments, and BeiLing got more complaints. BeiLing felt sad and jealous. He was afraid Mom didn't love him as much as BeiBei. That made BeiLing angry. When Mom was tired or busy, BeiLing could always get her attention by poking BeiBei. But as he grew older, he found a better way. He'd tease BeiBei or take his toy. He'd push his brother, and then call to Mom that

BeiBei had hit him. It was a relief to see Mom blame BeiBei for a change. Then Mom and Dad made a new plan. They sent both BeiBei *and* BeiLing to time-out. They kept reminding him, "We love you. When you want our attention or help, ask us. When you can control your body and use your words, you won't get a time-out. And we will all be in a much better mood."

❖ **Sleep.** There are several issues related to sleep.

❖ *Bedtime rituals.* Every night, BeiLing gets the same ritual: one story, two songs, and a five-minute back rub. Dad reads the *same* story night after night. Dad is *really* bored. But the same familiar story helps calm a restless mind and body. Any tiny change in the evening ritual caused upset and protest and more difficulty falling asleep.

❖ *Falling asleep.* For BeiLing, it's hard to lie still long enough to fall asleep. Active children find rhythmic motion is more soothing than lying still. As a baby, rocking or nursing did the trick. Not surprisingly, other youngsters gave up night feedings before BeiLing. (Eventually, Mom shortened night nursings and cut them out one by one. As she cut them out, Dad offered substitutes, like rocking or a pacifier.)

At bedtime, sucking a bottle or pacifier helped. After he turned three, the bottle became a problem. He couldn't stay dry when he drank so much. Mom looked for other kinds of soothing motion. She made up a quiet stretching song which she sang more and more slowly. BeiLing first stretched each arm and then each leg. When BeiLing turned three and a half, Mom suggested BeiLing sing the stretching song to himself or listen to a calm, familiar story tape on his tape player. Usually, BeiLing was then able to get to sleep by himself. But his dance of two steps forward, one back continued from time to time. When life is more frustrating, BeiLing sometimes needs help to fall asleep—especially during an illness or when starting a new school.

❖ *Getting ready for bed.* Active BeiLing never hears when Dad calls, "It's time to go to bed." So instead, Dad touches his shoulder, looks him in the eye and says, "When the timer rings, it will be time to get ready for bed." When the timer rings, Dad leads him to the bathroom where they brush their teeth together. Next, Mom goes with BeiLing to get his pajamas on. BeiLing Bluebird does better with a team effort. It doesn't matter that other children his age can get ready for bed by themselves.

❖ *Nightmares.* BeiLing sometimes has bad dreams. He dreams that he needs Mommy and can't find her, or that Mommy is on the other side of a river in a storm. As BeiLing grew, he sometimes dreamed that Mommy had died. He missed Mommy terribly! Because of BeiLing's temperament, he depends on Mom more than other children his age. BeiLing is genuinely afraid of losing her. Of course, when the household is stormy with anger, BeiLing does lose his warm connection with Mom—for a little while. After such nightmares, Mom reassures BeiLing that he is loved. They talk about ways BeiLing can ask for help, and things he can do while waiting for Mom. Mom also hugs BeiLing and tells him, "I'm going to live a long, long time."

❖ *Too excited to sleep.* BeiLing's parents have gradually learned that he needs about two hours of "slow-down time" before bed. Otherwise, he's too excited to sleep. For BeiLing, baths are exciting, so baths moved to the morning. BeiLing loves to play chase with Dad. But because Dad gets home late during the week, he only plays chase on the weekends. When the family goes out for dinner, they go early so they can be home two hours before bedtime. Every child is different. High energy BeiShi needs only an hour of relative calm before bedtime, and she can fall right to sleep after a bath.

❖ *Too little sleep.* BeiLing needs a full night's sleep to handle tomorrow's frustrations. His neighbor, Tiganda, needs a full night's sleep to refill her tank of adaptation energy. Life is better for everyone when these children get enough sleep. When most children get tired, they go to sleep. Not so with high energy BeiLing Bluebird or intense, slow-adapting Tiganda Tiger. When BeiLing gets really tired, his engine speeds up. When Tiganda gets too tired, her intensity goes up, and the transition to sleep gets harder. When these children don't get enough sleep, the days are filled with fussing and tears. BeiLing's usual energy turns into frantic activity. Having to wake them in the morning is a sure sign they haven't yet had the sleep they need.

Seeing this pattern, BeiLing's parents started evening slow-down and the bedtime ritual a little earlier each night. Within two weeks, BeiLing was waking up on his own in the morning. The days became much easier. Several months later, he again became overtired. So on Saturday, they made sure he got plenty of extra exercise in the afternoon. That evening, they started evening slow-down and the bedtime ritual early. Again, his behavior and mood improved the next day. During holidays, BeiLing and Tiganda were so excited, they needed extra time to calm down. So their parents started the evening slow-down and bedtime a little early. At times of stress, as when Grandma was sick or when starting a new school, it's especially important for BeiLing and Tiganda to get enough sleep.

✦ *Waking during the night.* All children (and adults) have sleep cycles—falling asleep, deep sleep, dreams, then waking or almost waking. Cycles usually last about one and a half hours and repeat through the night. Because BeiLing wiggles so much, he completely wakes up at the end of many cycles. Cousin BeiShu, who is active and sensitive, wakes if she gets too hot or too cold, hears a noise, or if she turns and bumps against the wall. Her bedroom is very dark, so Dad put up a night light. Now she can tell where she is when she wakes during the night. It's hard for parents to have a child who wakes frequently during the night.

✦ **Stuttering.** For a time, when he was learning to talk, BeiLing stuttered. It was worse when he was tired or excited. His thoughts moved faster than his mouth. Then he got frustrated because people didn't understand him. The more frustrated he got, the worse the words came out. Because Mom is high in energy, she began to finish sentences for BeiLing. But his doctor said, "BeiLing doesn't need help going faster. He needs help slowing down." So instead, Mom said, "I have time to listen to you, BeiLing. There is time to speak slowly." Mom took deep breaths to remind herself to slow down.

✦ **Temper tantrums.** When BeiLing was a baby, Mom and Dad made his frustrations go away. They fed him when he was hungry and soothed him when he was tired. But around eighteen months, they sometimes refused to help him. When he wanted to eat the dog's food, they put the dish out of reach. And they wouldn't let him splash water out of the bathtub.

BeiLing had moved to a new stage of development. His parents' new job was to limit some of his actions. In the past, when BeiLing cried, his parents came to the rescue and made frustration go away. Now they calmly said, "That food is for the dog. Your food is over here." BeiLing got angry that Mom and Dad didn't help him as they had before.

These were his first and necessary lessons that he and Mom are separate. They have different needs. BeiLing cried in pain and anger at this feeling of separation—feeling he had lost his connection with his parents. Then his crying turned to angry screams of a temper tantrum.

Mom talked calmly and held him if he wanted to be held, but did not change her mind. Because the rules stayed the same, BeiLing learned them more easily.

✤ **Testing limits and rules**. BeiLing gets frustrated and quits on jobs that aren't important to him—like getting dressed in the morning. But when it's something *BeiLing* wants, he gets frustrated when people try to stop him. His attention locks in to what he wants. BeiLing gets upset and asks over and over for what he wants. All his "wanting" energy shifts from wanting to see his friend to "blowing down" the resistance. BeiLing has lots of energy to keep asking.

At first, his parents didn't stand firm in these storms. They changed their mind and gave in. So BeiLing learned to complain more in order to get his way. His parents realized they needed a better way. When BeiLing asked for something, they said, "Let me think a minute." They took time to decide what was best. Then when they answered, "Yes" or "No," they were sure of their answer. Now it was easier to stand firm in the storm. Gradually, BeiLing learned that blowing harder didn't work.

✤ **Toilet training**. A bird doesn't stop flying because of a few rain-drops. BeiLing Bluebird doesn't want to stop to go potty. Besides, with diapers, Mom took care of everything. BeiLing was saved the frustration of all the details. Not surprisingly, BeiLing toilet trained later than other children.

Mom knew it was better to be patient than to get into a battle of wills. So she waited until BeiLing showed signs of interest. Sometimes Mom said, "When you are able to use the potty, I will have less work. I'll have more time to spend in the park with you." When BeiLing began to show interest, they broke the process into small, easy parts. Mom expected the dance of two steps forward, one step back. How well it went depended on how much frustration BeiLing was feeling in other areas. When BeiLing did use the potty, Mom took him for extra trips to the park and encouraged his effort. This helped BeiLing feel close to Mom in a different way than having his diaper changed. Gradually, BeiLing used the potty more and more often.

✤ **Trouble, attracted to**. Sometimes it seems that BeiLing *looks* for ways to annoy people. He tickles, teases, interrupts, repeatedly does things he knows he's not to do. He turns the bathroom faucet on full force, locks Dad out of the car, runs off and hides the house keys. Mom became a constant nag—"BeiLing, don't . . ." Under her breath,

Mom called him BeiLing the Bug, because he was always bugging people. As Mom learned about temperament, she kept track of when BeiLing was most annoying. Usually it was near the end of the day. BeiLing was tired from a full day of frustrations. The easy thing to do was to annoy someone. Then an adult would take over and tell him what to do next. When his mom understood this pattern, she looked for ways to make BeiLing her assistant, rather than her enemy: "BeiLing, I need your help. Can you bring a diaper for the baby? Can you hold the dustpan for me? Can you wash these vegetables? Can you carry these socks to the washing machine? Thank you so much for helping!" When BeiLing helped he felt important and close to his mom. Mom also collected ideas for easy, enjoyable things that BeiLing could do alone.

BeiLing's friend Brandon has the same temperament. Like BeiLing, he seems attracted to trouble. When he was four, he discovered that a way to get his teacher's attention was to touch girl's bodies or roll on the floor and look under their dresses. Fortunately, his teacher knew about temperament. She knew that the more she tried to stop him directly, the more he would push this limit. So instead, she kept him busy. She encouraged him to play running games with the other boys. She gave him his own recess ball, because he got frustrated playing ball with the other boys. When she saw him rolling on the floor, she asked him to run an errand for her. And she talked alone with the girls about staying quietly clear of Brandon. Because no one seemed to notice, Brandon stopped testing this limit.

Both BeiLing and Brandon tried using "bad words" when they turned four. Dad knew BeiLing was trying to upset him, so he completely ignored the bad words. Soon BeiLing stopped using them. Brandon's mom took a different approach. Each time, she said very calmly, "I can't understand that word. Talk to me with words I know."

❖ **Weaning**. BeiLing felt two very different ways about weaning. His active body didn't like staying in one place to nurse—he wanted to be up and moving. On the other hand, sucking calmed his body and made him feel safe. With days full of busy activities, he needed calm times for balance. Because he depended on Mom to help him with frustration, nursing helped to keep Mom nearby. Because nursing was important to BeiLing, his mom made the change very slowly. First, she dropped nursing after breakfast, and then after lunch, because that's when BeiLing felt most independent. Rather than going directly to a cup, he went from nursing to using bottles. Sucking is important to a child of BeiLing's temperament.

 **Words to Help Your Child Live with Frustration**

Parent	Child
If you lovingly tell your child:	Your child learns to say:
You like to work on a team.	*I like to work on a team.*
How can we break this into small parts?	*How can I break this into small parts?*
Let's take a short break.	*I can take a short break.*
This will get easier with practice. Everyone has to practice things.	*This will get easier with practice. Everyone has to practice things.*
Everyone gets frustrated. It's what you do next that counts.	*Everyone gets frustrated. It's what I do next that counts.*
You've done other things. You can do this, too.	*I've done other things. I can do this, too.*

Words to Help Your Child Live with High Approach

Parent	Child
If you lovingly tell your child:	Your child learns to say:
You love interesting, new things.	*I love interesting, new things.*
You don't like being bored.	*I don't like being bored.*
It's safer to look before you leap.	*It's safer to look before I leap.*

Words to Help Your Child Live with an Irregular Body

Parent	Child
If you lovingly tell your child:	Your child learns to say:
You get hungry at different times of the day.	*I get hungry at different times of the day.*
You get sleepy at different times of the day.	*I get sleepy at different times of the day.*

Words to Help Your Child Live with High Activity

Parent	Child
If you lovingly tell your child:	Your child learns to say:
You need lots of exercise each day.	*I need lots of exercise each day.*
You need a short break for some exercise.	*I need a short break for some exercise.*
Sometimes you think better when you're moving.	*Sometimes I think better when I'm moving.*
It's easier for you to sit if you let part of your body move.	*It's easier for me to sit if I let part of my body move.*

BeiLing Bluebird shares these behaviors with other children profiled in this book. For more help, see the pages noted here:

Discipline, pp. 70-71, 109   Sleep, pp. 57-58, 75-76
Eating out, pp. 111-112   Tests limits and rules, pp. 59-60

Walocka Whale
The Active, Slow-Adapting Child

Walocka is moved by huge, natural forces. Strong tides and great waves keep her constantly in motion. Even though she is sleek and beautiful, she cannot turn on a dime. There is something solid and unchanging about Walocka Whale. She is both constantly in motion and in charge of her own course. Sea captains respect her energy and power. They don't expect her to be different than she is. To sail safely with such great creatures takes time and planning ahead. All good sea captains plan before they venture out. That is the key.

Child shows: Activity, high and Adaptability, low

Keys to Living with the Active, Slow-Adapting Child

✤ **Adaptation energy, small tank of.** Cars have different-sized tanks for gasoline (energy). Small tanks need to be refilled more often than larger ones. Energy is required to make changes. Some people are born with smaller tanks of "adaptation energy" than others. Walocka Whale has a very small tank. She instinctively rations the little bit of adaptation energy she has. She demands Corn Chex instead of Wheat Chex, a ride from her dad to school as usual, and the story *before* the bedtime song. This saves adaptation energy for big things, like the new child in day care, a shopping trip, a substitute teacher, or Mom being sick with the flu.

Just as the gas tank runs low toward the end of a trip, adaptation energy runs low toward the end of the day. The lower the sun is in the sky, the lower Walocka's ability to get along with others. When her tank runs dry, she becomes frantic and disorganized. Small, unexpected events like a different route home from school because a road is closed, or an unexpected change in baby sitters, may cause a tantrum. When her adaptation energy is all gone, Walocka may demand something just for the sake of demanding. Then, when Mom gives in, she screams for the opposite. There seems no way of pleasing or calming her.

Because Walocka is slow to adapt, her parents work hard to keep afternoons and evenings as predictable and routine as possible. Sleep fills up her tank of adaptation energy. For the day to go smoothly, she needs a good night's sleep the night before.

❖ **Difficult transitions.** Walocka Whale is slow to adapt and high in energy. That means her energy pushes her out into life more—into more experiences that require bigger transitions. Walocka has to make big transitions from riding her bike wildly to lying in bed for a nap. To make changes, she has to manage a lot of energy. So her parents plan ahead for as many transitions as possible, going to bed, but also to coming to the table to eat, or getting in the car to go to the park.

Mom and Dad make transitions clear ahead of time. The more Walocka knows about what is ahead, the more easily she can make transitions. Before she could tell time, her parents used a visual timer of brightly colored oil and water to mark time limits. They turned daily events into routines that announce changes: "After lunch it will be nap time; after story time at day care, Mom will come pick you up; after breakfast we'll get in the car and go to the park; at the end of the video . . . " and so on.

At age three or four, her mom used a kitchen timer to announce changes: "In five minutes, we will . . . " or, "When the big hand of the clock gets to the top, we will . . . "

Around age four or five, Dad put a one-week calendar in Walocka's room: he put seven papers on the wall, with a picture to remind her of what usually happens each day. He used stick figures or symbols—green triangles for day care, or a different colored line when each parent was away.

✦ **Mind pictures.** Walocka is a natural planner. She lives with pictures in her head of what's going to happen next. Once she pictures peppermint ice cream in her head, chocolate will not do. Before she can change her behavior, she needs time to change the picture in her head. At age two, Mom tells her five or ten minutes ahead of time what is going to happen next. At three, Dad tells her as much as possible about the plan for the next day. When possible, they make only a few changes at a time. She needs time to get comfortable with one thing before adjusting to another. The more she knows about the future, the more secure and relaxed she feels.

✦ **Rules and rituals.** Walocka *loves* rules and rituals (once they are familiar). They help her know what will happen next; life is more predictable with fewer surprises. She thrives on the predictability of:

- eating out of the same blue bowl,
- drying her hair before her toes,
- sitting in the same place in the car,
- always taking a last turn on the swing before leaving the park,
- three kisses before going to sleep.

With age, the rituals become more complex, such as looking out at the thermometer before putting on a coat and eating French toast every Tuesday for breakfast. When Walocka turned four, family meetings became really important. When the family worked together to make plans and rules, there were fewer surprises.

 **Parent Care**

Invest time and effort for a deep look at yourself. Often the difficult job of parenting Walocka is made more challenging by having our own agenda—needing her to move before she's ready or swim to a place she is unwilling to go. Pushing a whale is hard work! Slow down; learn her agenda; plan ahead. Understand her needs and direction. Learn how to row with her flow. When Walocka does "blow," don't take it personally. Use these meltdowns as opportunities to learn and make a better plan for next time. As her parent, you are the waterway channel director. You monitor the ebb and flow of the tides, set clear guidelines and limits, and follow through on your commitments. Work with this great whale power by looking, whenever possible, for win-win solutions—ways you can both get what you need.

 Learning Style

Because of her activity level, Walocka learns by doing, not by watching. A whale wouldn't stop swimming and lie on the beach. It takes a lot of attention for Walocka to hold her body still. She learns more freely when she can move. For ages, humans survived by searching constantly for food and chasing after children. It's not surprising that many of us are not designed for sitting still. Direct Walocka's energy, don't try to stop it. Let her walk, or rock, or wiggle, or doodle while she learns. If you don't want her rocking back in her chair, give her a sturdy ball to sit on. Let her quietly chew gum or squeeze a ball of Silly Putty® under her desk. If her motion would disturb a sensitive child in the class, put her out of the line of sight of a sensitive child who is bothered by her motion. (A sensitive, slower-to-adapt teacher is more of a problem to deal with.)

✤ **Child care/Preschool.** Because she requires time to adapt, Walocka needs extra time to settle into a new child care or school situation. For her, there are three stages. First, she holds back a little and watches to see what goes on in this new place. She's putting new pictures in her head about how schools work. Second, she tests all the new rules, to see whether or not they will change. Third, when the new pictures are clearly in her head, and she settles in, she will be able to follow the new rules.

Common Behavior Issues

✤ **Attention, not paying enough.** Walocka is always on the go, living her busy life. And she takes in information primarily with her *body*, not her ears. Don't bother talking to her back. To get her attention, touch her shoulder, then make eye contact.

✤ **Cuddle, refuses.** It's hard to cuddle with a whale that is always on the move. Aunt Jenny's feelings were very hurt because Walocka wouldn't snuggle with her. Mom said, "She likes *you*, she just doesn't like being still." Mom advised, "Don't take care of her by holding her. Instead, take care of her by going places with her. Help her by telling her ahead of time what is going to happen. That's how she likes to be taken care of."

✤ **Danger.** It just takes a lot of effort for Walocka to hold her energy back. Furthermore, because she's slow to adapt, she resists new rules. And because she's slow to adapt it *takes time to build in new rules.* That's the bad news. The good news is that because she is slow to adapt, she thrives on routines, once they are firmly in place.

✤ **Discipline.** Active Walocka gets into more things than children who sit still. Can she climb the living room bookshelf? Can she open kitchen drawers to make a stairway to the counter top? How many toys can she take down from the shelf at once? How much water can she splash out of the tub? Beware of setting too many or too few rules for her. Parents who felt too controlled by their parents may enjoy her assertiveness and not want to set *any* limits. Other parents may not understand how much she needs to move and may set *too many* limits.

✤ *Testing limits.* Because Walocka is slow to adapt, it always takes a few weeks to learn a new rule. Mom needed to take her off Grandma's chair eight to twelve times and calmly put her on her own bed to jump. She finally has a mind picture that shows that her bed is the place to jump. Now she can remember.

Her friend Wakeetna is not so lucky. Like Walocka, he is slow to adapt. His parents always get angry when he can't remember rules right away. By the time he gets the new picture in his head, his parents have yelled at him eight times. He hates being yelled at, and he feels hurt and hopeless because he doesn't know how to stop their yelling. He feels resentful and now resists everything they say or ask.

✤ **Divorce/Loss.** Walocka's dependent side doesn't often show. High energy makes her look independent and ready to run her own life. So when her parents divorced, they thought she was handling the change just fine. But her stress came out indirectly, away from home. Walocka liked kindergarten. And because it had been going well before the divorce, she put even more energy into learning new games at recess, helping the teacher pass out projects, and serving snacks.

On the other hand, she started fighting more than ever with her two best friends. Any time friends disagreed with her, Walocka was afraid they would leave like Daddy had. Mom and her teacher told her that people can have different ideas and still get along. They reassured her, "Your friend isn't going to leave, like your Daddy did."

They knew that children with Walocka's temperament often don't talk a lot about their feelings. The kindergarten teacher asked Walocka to make sad pictures and angry pictures. Sometimes Walocka covered many pages with dark blue and purple scribbles. Mom read library books about divorce and told her often, "Daddy went away because he was upset with Mommy, not upset with you."

Not surprisingly, Walocka was more moody. It seemed that her tank of adaptation energy had shrunk. She got more upset than usual whenever plans and routines changed. Mom tried to keep as many things the same as possible. Once Daddy got settled in his new apartment, Walocka could visit him on weekends. To make things easier for Walocka, Mom and Dad agreed to keep rules the same in both homes.

✣ **Give-in/Get-tough cycle.** Because Walocka has so much energy, it's easy for her parents to alternate between too many rules and too few. This is the give-in/get-tough cycle. Here's what it looks like. When parents come home from work, tired, Grandma is ill, and the roof is leaking, life is too busy! Mom and Dad are too worn out to enforce the usual, reasonable rules. So Walocka gets out of control. Then Mom and Dad get overwhelmed by all the noise and trouble! They react with anger and punishment. For a few days they say "No!" to everything. Now they have been too angry and harsh, so they feel guilty. Besides, who would have to make Walocka follow all those rules? Walocka's energy requires a whole crew of rule keepers. Guilty and tired, her parents back off. Walocka gets out of control again, and the whole cycle starts all over.

For Walocka, the give-in/get-tough cycle means the rules keep changing. It is as though red means "stop" one day, and red means "go" the next. She gets confused. Every day she has to test every rule to see if it is on or off that day.

Here are ways out of the give-in/get-tough cycle:

Choose your battles. Make a *short* list of important rules and stick to them. Two might be "No hitting" and "Only the Nerf® ball can be thrown in the house." Child-proof thoroughly so that you aren't always saying, "Don't touch." Rather than fighting with Walocka to put on her shoes, hat, and jacket, Dad puts them in the car in case she wants them later.

Two yeses and a consequence. Walocka needs lots of help using her energy in positive ways. Tell her what she *can* do: "We can play chase in the family room and on the patio, but if you run in the living room, we have to stop," or, "You can roll the ball to your brother or bounce the ball to your brother, but if you throw it I have to put it away." This is distraction and redirection in action.

Enforce rules calmly and consistently. When Mom is calm, Walocka can pay attention to the problem, rather than being distracted by *Mom's feelings*. When Walocka does something unexpected, like jump in the airplane aisle, Mom asks herself, "Is this likely to happen again?" If so, she tries to think of a rule that will work in the long run. "Stand still!" won't work for long. Instead, she held Walocka while she thought for a moment. Then she said, "You can exercise in the aisle, but keep your feet on the floor and your hands to yourself. If you jump, you'll have sit in your seat." (At age three, Walocka had already learned lots of exercises, like deep knee bends and stretching down to touch her toes.) The more the rules stay the same, the *easier* they are for Walocka to remember.

Expect Walocka to test the rules. When Walocka throws a block, Dad says to himself, "Just like I expected, she's checking to see if the rule has gone away." Because Dad wasn't surprised or disappointed, it was easier to stay calm while he took the block away.

Avoid unnecessary temptations. Don't take busy Walocka to the antique store. Tired of so many toys on the floor? Divide them into three boxes. Put two out of reach, and rotate the boxes once a month. Want to avoid a meltdown because of the candy at the check-out stand? Mom shopped alone or went early in the day when Walocka is more able to handle frustration.

Provide enough sleep and snacks. Set the stage for better behavior by providing for basic needs. Walocka's mind and body will be better able to handle frustration.

Give opportunities for control. Let Walocka make choices whenever safe and reasonable: Which shirt to wear? Which park to play in? Which friend to play with? Which cup to drink from? Which story to listen to? However, don't give more choices than Walocka can handle.

❖ **Eating**. Walocka hated having a bib tied around her neck. It made her feel like the world was closing in on her. At her auntie's house, she never wore a bib. Auntie just changed her shirts more often than Mom did.

❖ *Eating out.* After a whole day of adapting, Walocka is in no shape to eat in a restaurant. After many tantrums and leaving restaurants without finishing, Mom and Dad decided to go out for brunch instead. At first, they only went to restaurants with a play area. As Walocka grew older, they went to a cafe that had booths. There was lots of room to wiggle. Only as she reached school age, did they go to restaurants where Walocka needed to sit in a chair.

✣ *Same foods.* For weeks at a time, Walocka ate the same foods day after day. When she thought about food, she saw pictures in her head of bananas and yogurt. One day, Mom put three peas on her lunch plate. They didn't look like food to Walocka; she didn't eat them. For the next five days, Mom put three peas on her plate. Mom always ate them before she took Walocka's plate away. On the sixth day, Walocka tried one. After a few more days, she began to like them. Mom had known to offer them at lunch time when Walocka was not so hungry or too tired. When she's really tired or hungry, she has no patience for new food. Mom kept only good, nutritious food in the house. She knew that over the course of a month, Walocka would eat a balanced diet.

At preschool, and sometimes at a party, Walocka tried new foods and even used a napkin. But when she got home she insisted on her same old favorites. Mom felt annoyed. Then she realized, "Walocka uses up her adaptation energy at school. When she comes home, she has very little adaptation energy left." Because there were always so many new and changing things in life, Walocka felt more secure when at least her food stayed the same, day in and day out, weekdays and weekends.

✣ *Self-feeding.* At six months, Walocka wanted to be in charge of her own meals and feed herself. Mom was happy with breast milk and finger foods. It made her life simpler. Dad put a plastic sheet under the high chair. Mom thickened yogurt with baby cereal, so Walocka could scoop it up with her fingers. Grandma felt differently. She liked feeding baby food because it gave her a special connection with her grandchildren. But Walocka repeatedly pushed Grandma's spoon away. She cried and banged on the tray for finger foods. Finally they found a compromise. Grandma gave her finger foods and a spoon to hold. Every once in a while, Grandma slipped a spoonful of bananas into Walocka's mouth. Grandma felt happy to be part of Walocka's life in this way.

✣ *Skipping breakfast.* Walocka is rarely hungry first thing in the morning. For her, waking up is a big transition that takes time. So she's not hungry until about 10 a.m. Mom packs a bag of cereal for her to eat in the car. At her preschool, she can eat breakfast whenever she's hungry.

❖ **Friends.** Because Walocka is on the move, she runs to any children who are playing nearby. But fitting in with other children doesn't come easily for her. All toddlers are self-centered, but children with Walocka's temperament appear especially self-centered. When another child in the play group reached out to share her toy, she would scream and sometimes bite. When this happened, Mom held her on her lap for a brief time-out. Walocka was always anxious to get off her mom's lap and play. As she learned to use words more, she hit and bit less.

❖ *Being the boss.* When Walocka is in charge, she doesn't have to spend as much of her adaptation energy adjusting to others. So she wants friends to play *her* way. She prefers to make the rules and tell others what to play. She likes playing with more adaptable children who are willing to let her be the boss. Of course, if they are younger, it's even easier for her to be the boss.

On the other hand, like BeiLing Bluebird, Walocka is attracted by the physical skill of older children. Being with older children is good for Walocka. She learns that when she screams and hits, they won't let her play. And they won't let her be the boss all the time. So she *has* to practice cooperation.

Because Walocka naturally wants to be a leader, her parents help her to learn to be a good one. Around age five, Walocka began to learn about being in control without being too bossy. Mom reported, "Ellen doesn't want to come play because she never gets to choose the games or make the rules." Mom suggested, "Sometimes, a good leader finds out where others want to go and then leads them there. What games does Ellen like to play? Or maybe Ellen will play with you if you use the timer and take turns being the leader. Or because you like to plan ahead, you might ask Ellen, 'What do you want to play after we finish this game?'" Mom then asked, "What else do *you* think might help, Walocka?"

Walocka needed more time to learn the give-and-take of friendship. During the learning process, there were friction and sparks. Because of the help she got, Walocka was learning how to be a better friend by the end of kindergarten.

❖ *Group size.* No one can know what is going to happen next in a large group of children. Therefore, Walocka feels much more comfortable with one or two friends she knows well. She can guess what is likely to happen next.

❖ *Time of day.* Mom noticed that Walocka did much better in a morning play group, when she still had lots of adaptation energy. Similarly, at age four, unstructured play with friends worked fine in the morning. But in the afternoon, it was better to have a definite plan ahead of time, so Walocka had less to adapt to.

❖ *Wanting to win.* Walocka likes rules because then she knows what to expect. She likes to make sure that other children follow the rules. Walocka also likes to win. Sometimes, when she is afraid of losing, she says, "I didn't hear *that* rule," or, "*That* rule is wrong!" Other children get upset and say she is lying. Sometimes the teacher suggests they play games where there are no winners or losers. Uncle Jed knows that it's hard to lose a game when you're young. He and Walocka played "Candyland" or "Chutes and Ladders." He would ask, "Do you want to play game rules or Walocka rules?" When Walocka made the rules, she *always* won. Some days, she felt able to play the game rules.

❖ **Lying.** One day when Walocka was four, Mom took her Christmas shopping. Walocka ran down an aisle and bumped an ornament off the shelf. She felt very uncomfortable that something bad had happened suddenly. She told her mother, "Santa Claus flew by and broke it!" Mom knew Walocka couldn't make sudden changes, so she picked up the ornament and paid for it. That night she said, "I need help paying for the Christmas ornament that got broken. Think about how you might help me." When Mom asked the next morning, Walocka gave her back some allowance money. Mom thanked her. Working with Walocka's need for adaptation time was more effective than telling her not to lie.

❖ **Talks too much or too loudly.** Because Walocka has so much energy, her voice is loud, like the roar of the ocean. Learning to talk more quietly is a slow process. Mom and Walocka practice by taking turns using loud, outdoor voices and quiet, indoor voices. Mom praised Walocka when she remembered her quiet voice.

Walocka hates to hear Mom say, "Don't talk so loud!" When Walocka needs a reminder, Mom silently puts a finger to her lips or begins to whisper. Because Walocka has to listen carefully, it helps her remember. When Walocka yells at Dad, he says calmly, "I can't hear you when you yell," and waits for her to talk more quietly.

Because of her high energy, Walocka has a lot to say. Sometimes Mom says, "I can't listen right now. I'm listening to the words in my own head." Walocka may continue talking, but at least Mom has said that she can't listen.

✦ **Trips, terrible.** After a visit to Grandma and Grandpa at Christmas and Disneyland during the summer, Mom never wanted to go on another trip with Walocka! Walocka had so much energy that she charged out into new places. By the second day, she had run out of adaptation energy. The third day was one meltdown after another. Mom and Dad decided to plan differently: they would keep afternoons easy and bedtime regular. After two days at Disneyland, they would go to a beach or park for the rest of the vacation so there weren't new rules every day. They would tell Walocka about plans and rules ahead of time. The next trip went much better.

Words to Help Your Child Live with High Activity

Parent	Child
If you lovingly tell your child:	Your child learns to say:
You need lots of exercise each day.	*I need lots of exercise each day.*
You need a short break for some exercise.	*I need a short break for some exercise.*
Sometimes you think better when you're moving.	*Sometimes I think better when I'm moving.*
It's easier for you to sit if you let part of your body move.	*It's easier for me to sit if I let part of my body move.*

Words to Help Your Child Live with Low Adaptability

See *Tiganda Tiger,* page 81.

Walocka Whale shares these behaviors with other children profiled in this book. For more help, see the pages noted here:

Danger, pp. 88-89
Discipline, pp. 70-71, 88-89, 109
Eating, pp. 90

Sleep, pp. 75-76, 98-100
Toilet training, pp. 78-79
Weaning, pp. 80

The Bear Cub Combo
The Active, Intense, Easily Frustrated, Slow-Adapting Child

Imagine the darting speed of a bird combined with the intensity of a prowling tiger and the powerful determination of a whale. When the temperaments of BeiLing Bluebird, Tiganda Tiger, and Walocka Whale all combine in one small body the result is the Olympic Challenge of Parenting. We call these human tornadoes the Bear Cub Combo. They are tossed by an internal storm of racing energy and a crowd of powerful feelings, including instant frustration.

One cub, Commotion, is cautious. He fiercely defends his familiar homeland. He wants his same food and the same forest paths. His sister Comeback, who is very high in approach, always races off to explore what's new or far away. Her parents are forever calling, "Comeback!" The cubs aren't *trying* to be difficult, but they crash against others again and again because 1) they have so much energy, 2) they are frustrated by difficulty and boundaries, 3) they are slow to adapt to the world around them, and 4) the more intense their feelings, the less they are able to change.

Hold your hats, everyone! Look back into your family tree to see where these traits came from. Chances are you can find some adults who have learned over a lifetime how to live with some of these traits. Take life one day at a time. Other adults rarely understand or appreciate the difficulty of your job. You deserve the gold medal for parenting under fire!

Child shows: Activity, high; Intensity, dramatic; Frustration reaction, easily discouraged or frustrated; and Adaptability, low

 Keys to Living with the Combined Challenging Temperaments

✤ **Plan ahead and step in early to *prevent* trouble.** Don't buy light-colored carpets. If possible, do your weekly shopping without taking your Bear Cubs. If Commotion has trouble putting shoes on, offer help *before* he gets upset, or let him go barefoot if shoes aren't really necessary. If Comeback has trouble peeling bananas, hand one to her already peeled. If the party is turning into a disaster, grab the twins and leave early.

Learning Style

Commotion and Comeback are active, intense, and easily frustrated. Both cubs share learning issues with their neighbors Tiganda Tiger, BeiLing Bluebird, and Walocka Whale. All people learn best when they feel calm and interested. Both Commotion and Comeback feel anxious when learning is difficult. In addition, curious Comeback is always thirsty for new things and quickly bored with the familiar. For her, the learning path, between anxiety on one side, and boredom on the other, is a *very narrow path*. Finding learning situations which suit her temperament is very important.

Common Behavior Issues

✤ **Cries when greeted by parents.** Commotion and Comeback often cry when Mom comes to pick them up at day care. They cry because the end of the day is harder for them, her arrival means another transition, and because all of their feelings are strong.

✦ **Dislike of new things.** Despite his high energy, Commotion is cautious around *new* things. It will take him time to get used to new experiences and people. Comeback, on the other hand, is eager to explore everything.

✦ **Temper tantrums.** Because the Bear Cub Combo have both high energy *and* high intensity, their tantrums are usually louder and longer than other children's. Because they are both slow to adapt and get easily frustrated, they have tantrums more *often* than others.

> The Bear Cub Combo share behaviors with three other children profiled in this book. Rather than repeat *all* the information here, read Chapters 8, 9, and 10. All parents with children like the Bear Cub Combo are going to be greatly helped by reading these chapters. You will need many skills and much understanding of the ways in which temperament affects the behavior of your child in order to survive and enjoy your offspring's childhood. Your child, too, needs to learn many skills to cope with his or her temperament and reach maximum potential.

Try out all the ideas in the relevant chapters to see what works for you and your child. Seek help from a temperament counselor or other qualified person if you need support. Good luck to all!

Temperament Poster

Copy this chart, and fill it in for all family members. Post it where you can refer to it easily and often as you make parenting decisions—on the refrigerator, the bedroom door, the car dashboard, etc.

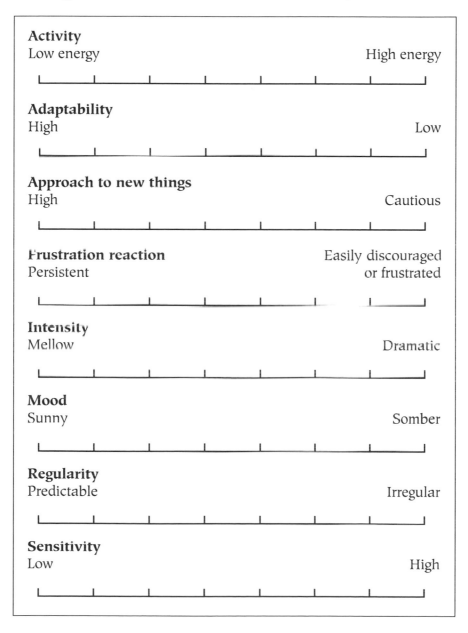

Activity
Low energy   High energy

Adaptability
High   Low

Approach to new things
High   Cautious

Frustration reaction   Easily discouraged
Persistent   or frustrated

Intensity
Mellow   Dramatic

Mood
Sunny   Somber

Regularity
Predictable   Irregular

Sensitivity
Low   High

Other Interesting Books

For adults

Baby Signs: How to Talk with Your Baby Before Your Baby Can Talk by Linda Acredolo, Ph.D. and Susan Goodwyn, Ph.D. Chicago: Contemporary Books, 1996.

Help! The Kids Are at It Again: Using Kids' Quarrels to Teach "People" Skills by Elizabeth Crary. Seattle: Parenting Press, Inc., 1997.

Highly Sensitive Person, The: How to Thrive When the World Overwhelms You by Elaine N. Aron. New York: Birch Land Press Book, Carol Publishing Group, 1996.

Know Your Child: An Authoritative Guide for Today's Parents by Stella Chess, M.D. and Alexander Thomas, M.D. Northvale, N.J.: Aronson, 1996.

Living with the Active Alert Child: Groundbreaking Strategies for Parents by Linda S. Budd, Ph. D. Revised edition. Seattle: Parenting Press, Inc., 1993.

On the Safe Side: Teach Your Child to Be Safe, Strong, and Street-Smart by Paula Statman. New York: Harper Collins, 1995.

Raising Your Spirited Child: A Guide for Parents Whose Child Is More Intense, Sensitive, Perceptive, Persistent, Energetic by Mary Sheedy Kurcinka. New York: HarperCollins, 1991.

For children

Feelings for Little Children series by Elizabeth Crary and Shari Steelsmith. Seattle: Parenting Press, Inc., 1996. Four books:
When You're Happy and You Know It
When You're Shy and You Know It
When You're Mad and You Know It
When You're Silly and You Know It

Other resources

Formal temperament analysis through Dr. James Cameron's website at http://www.preventiveoz.org. Parents can compare their child's temperament with other children's. Gain insight into what is moderate or extreme.

Growing Child. Monthly child-development newsletter. Subscriber gets the issue each month that coincides with child's age. Growing Child Publications, Lafayette, IN. Call 800-927-7289.

Index

Order these books for quick ideas

Tools for Everyday Parenting Series

Illustrated. Paperback, $11.95 each; library binding, $18.95 each

These books are geared for new or frustrated parents. Fun to look at and fun to read, they present information in both words and cartoons. They are perfect for parents who may be busy with school, jobs, or other responsibilities and who have little time to read.

Magic Tools for Raising Kids, by Elizabeth Crary

Parenting young children is easier and more effective with a toolbox of useful, child-tested, positive tools. Learn what to do, how to do it, and what to say to make raising lovable, self-confident kids easier.

128 pages, ISBN 978-0-943990-77-4 paperback

365 Wacky, Wonderful Ways to Get Your Children to Do What You Want, by Elizabeth Crary

Young children share certain behaviors that are calculated to drive parents crazy. Here are hundreds of practical (and sometimes zany) ideas to help parents cope.

104 pages, ISBN 978-0-943990-79-8 paperback

Ask for these books at your favorite bookstore or library, or call toll free Independent Publishers Group at 1-800-888-4741. VISA and MasterCard accepted with phone orders. Complete book catalog available on request.

Parenting Press, Inc., Dept. 801, P.O. Box 75267, Seattle, WA 98175
www.ParentingPress.com

Book distribution for Parenting Press in the United States and Canada by Independent Publishers Group. www.ipgbook.com

Prices subject to change without notice.